Morningside Memories

Volume 2

Published by Morningside Heritage Association
15 Dalhousie Terrace, Edinburgh EH10 5NE

First published 2003

ISBN 0 9544850 0 9

Printed in Great Britain by Nimmos Colour Printers

Contents

Introduction

In 1986 the Morningside Association, the Morningside Heritage Association and Morningside Community Council collaborated in the production of a booklet entitled *Morningside Memories*, based on the reminiscences of elderly people living in the area. The contents of the booklet spanned the years from just before the First World War to the beginning of the Second World War. The publication proved to be most successful. Almost 1,500 copies were sold and, for a time, it was listed among the 'top ten bestsellers' in its category.

As the millennium approached, members of the Morningside Heritage Association (MHA) decided that it was now time for a second volume, bringing our thoughts and memories of Morningside up to date from the years of the Second World War to the end of the twentieth century.

The contents of the booklet are based on the reminiscences of men and women who have spent part or most of their lives in the Morningside area – life as people remember it. The booklet covers childhood which, although sometimes darkened by the shadow of war, was a time of freedom to roam from the Braidburn Valley to the Blackford Hills; the days of war service or first jobs; visits to the cinema and dancing at the Plaza Ballroom; parties and weddings; setting up home in the austere post-war years; advances in medicine; and finally the changes we are observing in the Morningside of today.

Oral history, which depends on an individual's own recollections and perceptions of an event, may contain some inaccuracies but, nevertheless, this is life as we remember it in Morningside.

Acknowledgements

The Morningisde Heritage Association editorial team would like to thank the 37 contributors to this volume of *Morningside Memories* for the wealth of material they provided, the time they gave and the fun we shared. They are: Pat Bruce, Joan Burnet, Derek Cameron, Alice Clark, Anna Cunningham, Mary Cunningham, Audrey Currie, Norma Dale, Kay Ellis, Catherine Glen, Rosemary Harvey, Archie Hay, Margaret Howat, Bill Hunter, Dorothy Lakie, Sheila Logie, Mary Lugton, Catherine McDonald, Mairi Macdonald, Margaret McGregor, Tibbie Mackenzie, Catriona Macnaugton, Marion Mack, Val Manning, Gwen Menzies, Jim Mitchell, Irene Montgomery, Anne Morham, Marjory Paul, Mary Peter, Elizabeth Reid, Florence Reynolds, Rosemary Rodgerson, Muriel Rudd, Maureen Smith, Marjorie Whitton, Johanna Wright.

The following people kindly lent us photographs to be reproduced in the booklet: Malcolm Cant Publications, Phyllis Cant, Margaret McGregor, Marjory Paul, W. Ovens.

We are most grateful to Stanley Douglas and the Kirk Session of Morningside Braid Church for allowing our regular group meetings to be held in their premises.

We have been very fortunate to receive grants from Age Concern, which helped us with the initial cost of stationery, tapes, etc., and also from our Local Development Committee of Edinburgh City Council to meet the cost of printing. We are very grateful for these.

We should also like to thank Malcolm Cant and Charles Smith for their interest and advice, and Mairi Sutherland, Mike Storie and students on the BA (Hons) Publishing and MSc Publishing programmes at Napier University, School of Communication Arts, who helped us prepare the booklet for publication.

MHA editorial team: Elizabeth Deans-Davies, John Duffus,
Jennifer Meiklejohn, Marjorie Wood
Morningside Heritage Association 2003

Chapter 1

Childhood

It was perhaps to be expected that members of our group would have many memories of their childhood and these feature vividly in these reminiscences.

School

First Kiss
by Tibbie Mackenzie

I was just turned eleven
And glued to a book
When he suddenly kissed me
And gie'd me a look.

'Do you love me?' he said.
Seemed rude to say, 'No.'
So I lied through my teeth
To wee Duncan Munro.

Then I gie'd it him straight.
'Nae mair o' yer tricks
'Cos I'm no' for gaun oot
Wi' a Primary six.'

Morningside School and Boroughmuir School

'I remember Morningside School. When my sister and I came back after being evacuated we had to do a test. I think when you went in the girls' door, the classroom was there; it was like steps, the desks were layered.'

'Oh that's right, they were tiered.'

'Well, I remember that particular room. Maybe the reason is I was asked to spell SCHOOL and I left out the H. I said to my sister, "How do you spell SCHOOL?" and she wouldn't tell me. I spelt it SCOOL and I knew it was wrong. There must only have been the two of us in that classroom and that's maybe why I remember.'

'I always remember these seats away up to the top of the classroom and if you were the best you were at the very top: back seat, left-hand side. And if you were the worst you were down at the right-hand side of the bottom row. We had a test every week and you picked up your bag from your desk and then you moved to wherever you were put. And if you were lucky you were moving the right way and, if not, you weren't.'

'I don't think I moved!'

'Do you remember we had to march in to the piano in the mornings and at lunchtime as well? We all had to line up in the playground, the boys in one and the girls in the other, and then they played the piano and we all marched in.'

'They don't do that now.'

'I remember the Coronation celebrations we had; it would be in '53, just in my Qualifying year. We were all taken up to Braidburn Valley; that was used a lot – I think it still is – if you were having outdoor pursuits.'

'Not so much now, but you did the school sports there in those days as well.'

'For the Coronation you were given flags and I think we all got a mug. I don't know what happened to my mug.'

A contributor who no longer lives in the area asked:

'I was at Morningside School; is it still there?'

'Oh yes it is – bulging at the seams in fact.'

'I can tell you two of my teachers' names. I had a Miss Brydon and a Miss Hunter; she took us to our Qualifying. Miss Hunter was a very good teacher. I was there from '40 to '47. Both my sister and I went on to Boroughmuir. That was a very good school. Mr Carswell was the Head, he came while I was there. I went to Boroughmuir in '47 and my wife went to Boroughmuir in '47; that's where we met.'

Did you go up to Bruntsfield School for swimming when you were at Morningside?

'Yes I did. Miss King was the teacher and I left because she pushed me in and I swallowed half the pool and I never went back. I was terrified and I can't swim to this day, and I blame Helen King. She was teaching us to dive in and I was standing at the edge of the pool, "Get in boy" and she just pushed me in. Does Bruntsfield still have a pool?'

'Oh yes, and still in use'.

'Bruntsfield was built in 1895 with a swimming pool in it and Sciennes, Abbeyhill and Dalry. That was very forward looking in the 1890s.'

'Boroughmuir was very lacking in facilities for a senior secondary school.'

'Have you been back since they built over the gym? They've made a lovely hall above on the second floor level – you know there was that empty space and it's a beautiful assembly hall now. It has made the inside of the building darker but it was a sensible use of the space there.'

This evoked another memory shared by many Boroughmuir pupils. 'I remember we always seemed to get gym the first period after lunch and there was carrots and custard all over the floor [school dinners were served in the gym], and the gym teacher would say, "Now I want you all down flat on your backs" and you'd wander around trying to find a clean space to lie down and he'd shout, "Where are you going, boy?"'

Was Mr Ronchetti the boys' gym teacher when you were there?

'Yes, that's right, and Taylor was the assistant. Oh I enjoyed Boroughmuir but – again – it didn't have any facilities. I mean everybody hoofed it out to Meggetland for rugby, football, sports and hockey and it's a long way out too! You didn't get a lift or anything, you walked along the canal bank or you got a tram out and I used to walk home to Morningside via George Watson's.

There was a lane at the bottom of Myreside that ran along the railway bank; I don't know if it's still there.'

Cranley School and James Gillespie's School

'I was at Cranley School in Colinton Road and we walked to school every day and back. A school friend and I used to go together when we were five. We trotted off, just the two of us. I think my sister took me about once but decided I was rather a nuisance.'

'Big sisters are like that!'

Can you remember much about your early schooldays there?

'I remember being very annoyed with a little boy because I wanted to get to school before him and because he lived across the road in Polwarth he could see me coming down the Drive and he was in before me every time.'

So there were little boys at Cranley too?

'Yes, in the Kindergarten. I was never in the big school in Colinton Road because by the time I got to the big school we were in Spylaw Road. The Kindergarten stayed in Colinton Road.'

'I went to James Gillespie's and we too walked to school. One little girl in my class had a sister in the class of an older friend and they used to take us to school when fathers or mothers deposited us at Morningside Station. Most of the dads and business people went by suburban railway to town – 11 minutes from Morningside Station to Waverley. Father always used to speak about the zone ticket – it was 1s 6d a week.'

St Peter's School

With plans in progress to rebuild St Peter's school in Falcon Gardens, a group of former pupils recall their schooldays there in the 1940s and 1950s.

'I can remember what I wore on my first day at school. My mum had made me a green and white check kilt and a black sweater.'

'I remember I had a new navy blue nap coat and I wouldn't take it off. Sister Teresa tried to take it off. I even sat and ate my lunch with it on, I wouldn't take it off!'

'I always wore a box pleated gym tunic and a white or blue blouse and eventually the navy blue and yellow striped tie. My first classroom was in the small room behind the Church; the Parish room.'

'I remember being in P1 in the Parish room and there was only one tiny little toilet for everyone, no wash basin and there were lots of accidents! The main school only had four classrooms and a balcony and they thought it was easiest if P1 was in the Parish room. There was a hall in the main school overlooked by the balcony and school dinners were served in the hall.'
'And as well as the dinners we got milk every day. The P7 boys got to deliver the crates to each room. I was the "milk monitor" and got to put the straws in the bottles.'
'Yes you got one little paper straw and if you chewed it up and couldn't suck with it – too bad!'
'When it was playtime we were taken over from the Parish room in a crocodile, two by two, holding your friend's hand to the playground.'

'The nuns who taught in the school lived in the convent adjacent to the school building. They were Sisters of Charity of the Order of St Vincent de Paul. They wore heavy serge robes, ankle length, and big swan hats. I have never met anyone who was intimidated by them.'
'Sister Philomena, the Headteacher, used to come into the playground and ca' the rope for the skipping games.'
'Sister Teresa always took the baby class and I remember the big box of dolly mixtures she kept to hand out as rewards.'
'Another thing I remember about Sister Philomena, she had a large rosary which hung from her pocket and when we were little we used to hold on to it in the playground and she would twirl us round on it.'
'The youngest curate used to come over and play football with the boys.'
'Sister Teresa used to read us a story on Friday afternoon as we sucked our dolly mixtures. I remember once, she was reading Peter Pan and when she imitated one of the characters her false teeth flew out. We all laughed so much, as she did too, that she could not go on with the story so she sent us all home early.'
'Do you remember playing on the banking at the rear of the school? There was a bank which sloped up to a boundary wall where large trees grew. A favourite game in autumn was to design little houses laying out the leaves as rooms, kitchens, hallways etc.

I don't think we ever got round to playing houses. We spent the whole playtime on the architectural design and by the next playtime the leaves had blown away.'

'When you were in P7 you could join the girls' club on a Friday evening run by the Sisters. I remember they took us on an outing to Dunfermline. It was pouring and the Sisters lifted their long robes to avoid the puddles. It was the first time I had seen their feet and I was shocked at their shoes; they were all down at the heel and split at the back. Their feet must have been soaking.'

'Do you remember Mrs Paterson's sweet shop, just beside the Library? We were allowed to go out of the playground, across Morningside Road to the shop for sweeties during the lunch hour.'

'Yes and we used to go to the Library then too. You were allowed two tickets and I would look for two Enid Blyton adventures or two Chalet School stories. If you found three on the shelf you would hide one behind the other books and hope to find it when you went back. But you never did!'

'Yes we had lots of freedom. It was very different when my own children went to St Peter's in the 1970s. The playground, the buildings and the curriculum had all changed. The famous rear wall had been moved back and the surface flattened. New classrooms had been added. Music lessons now included instrumental tuition and the children put on song and dance shows in the Churchill Theatre. There was far more sport too; inter scholastic athletics, football, netball and swimming. Of course much of the coaching is done by volunteers. There was no leaving the school grounds to visit local shops etc. and sweeties were no longer considered a suitable reward for any achievement.'

'Good times! Bad times! Which was which?'

Other school memories

'Boroughmuir and Darroch were the local secondary schools where you went after Morningside. Later one half of Morningside went up to Firrhill and the other half came down to Boroughmuir. Darroch is closed now. Gillespie's was part fee paying and some went there. And we walked all the time, not getting buses like nowadays.'

'No, that's true.'

'The other day I went down Leamington and I passed what used to be the school house. [The house was used by Darroch for some of the domestic science lessons.] If you were doing domestic science you went to this house and you kept house. I learned a lot there. We had an afternoon tea party for our mothers to come and my mother had a hat with a thing on it the same colour of felt as the hat with gold bits on it and I saw this gold thing passing the window and I thought, "Here's my mother coming." And as usual she embarrassed me by telling the teacher of my one failing at baking and making tablet. I made tablet and put twice as much sugar in it. And she trotted out this story!'

South Morningside School Reunion 1992

The school reached its centenary in 1992 and various events were held with the present-day pupils during the year. In November a former pupils' reunion was held in the halls of Morningside Braid Church. About 150 past pupils and teachers attended and an interesting time was had by all seeking out former school friends and wondering whether we would recognize each other.

After an introduction by the organiser, Mrs Elizabeth Notman (née Clanahan), who has since died aged 101 in 2001, was invited to cut the centenary cake duly iced and ribbonned in the school colours. Mr Gilbert Main and Mr David Mitchell (both now deceased) were among our other older brigade of pupils. Mrs Jeannette Perry, Headteacher at the school, was a guest.

Many photographs were taken during the evening and slides shown of the school past and present by Mr Bill Smith and a lot of animated discussion of the memories of us all took place. A buffet supper was then enjoyed. Pictures and mugs as mementos of the occasion were bought.

Mr Bill Smith also mounted a display of photographs of the evening in the Library, which was viewed by many locals.

With the balance of proceeds of the evening, a presentation was made to the school early the following year of a multi-instrument weather centre, together with a portable, electronic thermometer / hygrometer and also a digital world map clock telling the time in different countries.

Marjory Paul (née Riley), Organiser

Paper rounds

Did you have any after school jobs?

'I delivered papers in the morning for a wee while for the paper shop up at Churchill – Cruickshank's.'

So you would have to be up there early?

'Yes, I did the tenements at Churchill, then I did round the back at Abbotsford and ended up at these flats in Colinton Road that I call old fashioned modern – you know where I mean – and they had a caretaker and I never got into those flats. I handed over the bundle of papers and he delivered them to the flats.'

Were they big houses in Abbotsford?

'Yes, and there was one had a dog and I was terrified to go in. I didn't do the job for very long!'

Do you remember what they paid you for it?

'No I don't. What I do remember is the people in the tenements were better tippers than the people in the big houses. Everybody in the tenements gave you something whereas everybody in the big houses didn't. You might get a big tip from one, but nothing from the two people on either side.'

Leaving school and first jobs

Can we talk about when you were leaving school and going into your first jobs?

'Well when you left school they sent you to the Youth Employment Centre in St Giles Street. If one of the teachers found out what you wanted to do, then you were sent there. Then if it was an office you wanted to go to they sent you to two or three offices. You got a little card to say who you were and that introduced you.'

How old were you then?

'Almost 16, we could all leave school at 15 but I stayed on for a 4th year to do extra commercial at Darroch which had a very good commercial department – it was well known for it. I remember Mr Burrell and Miss Rosie. We got a very good commercial grounding at Darroch. We had school magazines at that time and we used to get involved with printing the magazine and things like that and helping the Secretary in her office. So you got an idea of what it was like to take telephone calls or something like that.'

Did you go to night school when you first started work?

'Yes, I went to Boroughmuir Night School to carry on with the RSA exams. We took typing particularly and shorthand. We went on to do usually up to about 120 to 140 words a minute.

Recreation and youth organisations

What did you do in your free time at home and out of doors in these pre-television days after school and paper rounds etc?

'We listened to Radio Luxemburg nearly every night while we were doing homework. On a Sunday when we were all at home we used to play games such as Ludo, Snakes and Ladders, and it was just a fun day. Sunday school in the morning and you'd go out for a walk if it was nice, in the afternoon.'

'On Sunday you always went to your Granny's or your Auntie's.'

'Yes every Sunday – or at least it seemed like every Sunday – we set out to walk to where my Grandmother lived and that's where we had our Sunday tea.'

'We used to look for frog spawn over by Mortonhall Golf Course and gather it up in a jar and take it home and put it in a basin in the garden and watch the wee legs grow. We had to go down to the Braid Burn to get weed to feed them.'

'Children now are losing all the old street games we used to play endlessly – skipping and peevers and that sort of thing. We played so many games like "You can't cross the river" and "What's the time, Mr Wolf?" At our children's parties we played "The farmer's in his den" and "Pass the parcel" and things like that and I made the birthday cake with Smarties and Jelly Babies on it and they loved it.'

'Younger children still enjoy these games. I did Beavers, the boys were aged 6 to 8 and they enjoyed these games very much.'

'And there were Scouts and Guides and these overspilled into camping and hikes at weekends. There were school based activities when you were older; the drama club and the debating society as well as all the sports activities.'

'You were never allowed to play in the back green; that was for washing and drying clothes. You see, in Springvalley, there was never a car when I was a girl [war time] so we used to play rounders and peevers and "Kick the can" in the street, if we got away with it.'

'I used to cycle up to Fairmilehead and we used to play in the bluebell woods and take a picnic in the basket on your bike and after, you filled up the basket with flowers on the way back.'
'I remember we used to play a lot in the Braidburn Valley. We used to walk home to Fairmilehead from Morningside School. We had great detours round by Harwell's farm and all sorts of places.'
'We had so much more freedom. I remember as a youngster, my playground was the Braids – we just roamed the Braids. There was no fear of children being molested or attacked.'
'That's true, things were safer in those days, or at least they appeared to be.'
'I remember being on Blackford Hill and the gorse being on fire and seeing all the wee rabbits running out.'
Did you feed the ducks on the pond when you were wee?
'Oh yes and we had many a walk on Blackford Hill.'
'We always went up to Blackford Hill to roll our Easter eggs. Mother usually boiled them in cochineal and made them pink, or tea, which made them a sort of browny colour. We rolled them on the Sunday afternoon, after we had been to church and Sunday school.'

Sunday Prelude
by Tibbie Mackenzie

Church bells ringing, slow and insistent,
Matching the mood of our Sunday best shoes,
As we trudge with our pennies and neat folded hankies
To swell the collection and fill up the pews.

Mother and sisters 'way on ahead now,
Brother and I giving them room
As we scuffle our way past Gemmel's the dairy
And dark Canny Man's sabbatical gloom.

We slink round the corner at Morningside Laundry,
The rest of the family's through the Church gate.
My brother says, 'Here, I'm off to the Blackfords.'
And gives me his penny to put in the plate.

Guides, Scouts and Beavers have been mentioned before. Can you tell us more about these organisations?

'Well we were Guides and Brownies at Greenbank Church.'

Did you ever go camping?

'Oh yes indeed! Pinkie House Musselburgh Brownie Pack holidays were great fun. It was the very first Pack holiday in the whole of Scotland, May Corson (Brown Owl) was the first one qualified to take a Pack holiday.'

'I remember one time we went when I was a Pack Leader and we took with us four Brownies from the Grassmarket, a much more deprived area then, and they had a wonderful time. I was sent one day to Musselburgh, to buy one child a pair of sand shoes. They were terribly expensive – 1s 11d or something!'

'My Brownie days were over the war years so we didn't have any Pack holidays.'

'The first year of the war Greenbank Guides and Rangers went to Aberfeldy, to Glen Lyon, where we had a cottage. We had been allocated the Chalet in Switzerland in 1939 but of course it was cancelled and we never did get it.'

'I was in Braid Church Guides and there was this waste ground near the Priory, near where St Peter's school is. We made an oven thing and we cooked potatoes and stuff and kept them in this. It was a box with straw.'

'Like a hay box?'

'Yes, this was emergency cooking. If the Germans came and you were fighting, the Guides were going to be out there cooking for the whole street. We had vegetables because there were allotments along there. Some people were busy peeling potatoes and vegetables and others were boiling them and sticking them into these ovens.'

'The Cubs [in Braid Church] had a superb Pack. A. F. Ross was the Scout Master in the 1940s. He had a very good parents' group going and together they ran coffee mornings and things to create funds. Now that, during the war, was difficult. When he married and left, the Scouts just went downhill and the Boy's Brigade which was the 55th at St Matthew's (now Cluny Church) just picked everybody up. There were 60 or 70 boys in it, as I remember. The Smiths from Maxwell Street ran it. There was

Father, and Charlie did a bit, then Bill, and there was a chap McLaren and a David Dickson also from Maxwell Street. That was when I was a boy in the Company. It was a good going Company.'

'The BBs then had quite a big pipeband and we marched all along Princes Street on a Sunday to mark founder's day. The owner of the Canny Man – Kerr, or maybe his father – I'm going back to the late 1940s or 1950 – gave the BBs a set of bagpipes but instead of ivory they were silver, just as a token. Nobody knows to this day where those pipes are. They were valued at £200, which was a lot of money in those days.'

'Somebody will have them in their house and not even know where they came from!'

Did the BBs go camping?

'Yes we went twice, to Dunbar and Rothesay. Again, we had a Parents Association who raised money. You need a lot of money to take boys to Rothesay. Rothesay was a super camp – poured for the first three days! We generally went the first week of the Edinburgh Trades holiday and you'd probably find the camp site was going to be taken over by the Glasgow boys the following week. It was on farms, under canvas and we always had a cook and what have you. It was great – well, if you liked that sort of thing!'

A gentleman who had attended Morningside School and then Heriot's in the late 1920s and 1930s joined the reminiscence group one afternoon having travelled from Dundee to attend the funeral of Mr Sandy Ross, former Scout Master of the Troop at Braid Church. It says a great deal about Mr Ross that, after all those years, so many former Scouts attended his funeral (he was in his 90s).

This gentleman told us:

'There was a Scout reunion in 1994 to mark the anniversary of the formation of the 25th troop [at Braid Church] in 1919. It was organised by Catriona Reid, the Scout Leader in 1994 and I was very glad to come down and meet quite a number of old friends for the first time in many years. It was very well attended; I would say about 30 Scouts and 20 partners. There was a further reunion, an 80th, in 1999.'

You were married in Braid Church; did you meet your wife through the church?
'Yes my sister was Guide Captain here and my wife was one of her Lieutenants.'
This must have been a very active church?
'It was; there were so many Cubs that they had a waiting list and I couldn't get in here so I was sent up to the 48th Pack at North Morningside Church and did all my cubbing there. Then when I came of age for Scouts I came back to the 25th here. There was an annual Scout camp every summer and we always used to go away somewhere away from home. The first one I remember being at was at Beil Estate at Dunbar.'
How primitive was it, camping in those days?
'We didn't think it was primitive at all. Few of us had sleeping bags, you made your own up with blankets, a blanket roll, latterly you got a sleeping bag. You slept on ground sheets, which were rubber backed canvas, on the grass. In those days they were mostly bell tents and you'd have a horse-shoe shape with 5 or 6 of them round a camp fire in the middle. Each patrol had its own tent and each tent slept up to 8 people. Then there was the officer's tent where you had the Scout Master, the assistants and maybe one or two other helpers.'
And was the campfire kept alight all the time?
'No, it was allowed to die down at night. The next morning the Patrol on cook's duties had to get up early and light the campfire. The firewood had to be collected the night before and put in one of the tents so it was dry for the morning.'
Did you make 'damper' – flour and water?
'Flour and water, sugar or salt, – if your mother knew about it you got a little baking powder to make it rise a little. And you had porridge every morning.'
'And then some poor soul would have to clean the porridge pot!'
Did you take the food with you or did you buy it locally?
'Milk and eggs from the farmer, yes, bread from the local baker and the local butcher for your meat. The worst job of all was digging the latrines, with usually just a screen of sacking. That would be the first job that had to be done and putting up the tents.'

And who got the job of filling in the latrines afterwards?
'Well that was just one of the duties.'
What sort of activities did you have while you were there?
'Oh, what do boys do when they are out in the country? – played pirates, hide and seek in the woods, leavoi, and you'd go trekking and nature trails and things, climbing and swimming – plenty of activities and a sing song round the camp fire at night and if there were any other Scouts or BBs in the district you had combined sing songs.'
How did you travel in those days to Scout camp?
'You hired a lorry. The lorry came to Braid Church here and we loaded all the tents and stuff and the boys with their kit bags in the back. He took us, then said, "Right! I'll see you in two weeks time." Then he came back to take us home. Parents Day was the middle weekend, they were allowed to come to see if you were still living – to see if we had survived the camp cooking!'
Were there Gang Shows in those days?
'No I think Gang Shows started after the war.'
And did you go to Jamborees?
'I could never afford to go because they were always abroad, but somebody I was speaking to at the funeral this morning said he was one of the few to go to the Jamboree in Copenhagen in 1937. He was the only one from Morningside area who went.'

'We had Youth Fellowship in those days. When you got too old for the senior Bible Class you went on to the Youth Fellowship, that kept you together. We used to get all together and go for Sunday afternoon walks after church. It was more social than studying. It was a good way of meeting up with members of the opposite sex.'
'Yes especially if you went to a single sex school.'
'And you'd be well chaperoned?'
'Yes, very – and we had dances.'
These would be the sort of things parents would approve of?
'As long as it was in the church it was fine!'
'I think Greenbank Church was the most powerful in youth involvement.'
'That was through David Read.'
'That's right, David Read and Quest – now QII.'

[Rev David Read returned to his charge at Greenbank Church after war service and set up Quest, an organisation for young people. It too celebrated a 50th anniversary in 1995.]

Pranks

Can you remember any pranks you got up to?

'The sort of things as boys we used to do, was get calcium carbide – now that's the stuff that makes acetylene gas – and before the war it was common at the chemist's. We'd get a small tin, put a drop of water in it and a wee bit of calcium carbide, knock the lid tight down, then wait for it to go off BANG – hoping that someone was walking past!'

'The only thing I can think of is that my chum and I were playing at the Braid Burn and we thought we'd walk underneath the bridge. So we did. We managed to paddle underneath the bridge and when we got to the other side there was a lady standing outside her front door with a frying pan shaking it at us. We got the fright of our lives!'

Where had you come out?

'We must have come out into the garden of the cottage at the gate of what is now the Hermitage on Braid Road.'

'She must have been accustomed to children doing that and she was waiting for you.'

'We used to walk along the lane next to the Jordan Lane wall. I don't know if it is still possible, but you could walk right away along there – you maybe had to get on the wall occasionally – till we got to Sonny Jim, his house.'

'I think it's full of Japanese knotweed. You couldn't walk along there now.'

'Sonny Jim used to have bits of glass on his wall so you couldn't walk along it though we had a good shot at it sometimes. You could actually get out at Woodburn Terrace by walking along there.'

'Who was Sonny Jim?'

'Oh he was just a man in the street who disliked children. We were horrors anyway!'

Toys

What kind of toys did you have when you were young?

'Well in the war time you couldn't get new toys, you had to pass on things.'

'Clothes too.'

'I remember a very large Teddy bear, it was bigger than all of us. It went down through the family and it got more and more battered and dirtier.'

'Yes we had one like that too. It came from an older cousin to you and once you got too big, you had to hand it on to a younger cousin.'

'I remember my doll's pram being handed on to somebody else. I was lucky because I had an older sister and she had got things which were passed down to me.'

'I remember my brother having a thing you made with wheels off a pram – a guider they called it. I remember them building that; Dad and him building that.'

'The girl next door to me and I always took things together – the mumps, the measles and whatever and we had had one of these things just before Christmas and she got a sledge for Christmas and we actually got snow. We were just recovering and getting out to play and I can remember us yet, sitting on this sledge saying, "Don't come near us. We've got the mumps" so that nobody else could get a shot on the sledge and we pulled each other up and down Springvalley.'

'People used to go out on an old tin tray to sledge, didn't they?'

'When we had that snowfall a couple of winters ago I was coming down past the Braidburn Valley in the bus and it was a beautiful sight. It was covered with parents and children, all colourful, with sledges. I hadn't seen that for years.'

'We used to sledge down there – too bad if you steered into the burn!'

'The dangerous place to sledge was Blackford Hill because you tended to go into the bushes and you spent the next six weeks getting out the thorns.'

'And the other place was the Merchant's Golf Course or the Braids.'

'Winter was winter then.'

'And summer was summer. I remember we had beautiful summers then. We used to get a basin of cold water in the garden and put our feet in it and spray ourselves. The weather was gorgeous.'

Libraries

Did the library feature prominently in your lives?
'Oh yes, I enjoyed the Library. There was no television or anything. We used to go with my mother regularly every week to pick our books and carry them all the way back home.'
'There wasn't the choice of children's fiction that there is nowadays. I remember it was just one case in the main library. What were your favourites?'
'Enid Blyton and Angela Brazil.'
'Mine were the Chalet School stories by Elinor Brent Dyer, I loved those.'
'And the Katie books, I liked the Katie books.'
'And Anne of Green Gables – that was nice.'
'And Pollyanna.'
'We must all have been borrowing the same books one after the other.'
'I don't remember paperbacks. They were all hardbacked books in the library, quite dull looking actually, and you could only have two out at a time.'
'And you didn't dare forget to return them on time or you were fined. My brother was very bad for forgetting them and a postcard used to come. My mother thought it was a terrible disgrace. I think when we knew that there might be one due we used to try to get the postman before my mother saw the post. The fine wasn't very heavy, about 1 penny a week.'
'Yes, a penny.'
'But as you say, it was a terrible disgrace to the family.'
'Absolutely!'

A Morningside childhood

A former Morningside resident who now lives in Berwickshire wrote to us of her childhood.

I was born in Edinburgh in 1944 and lived at 1 Midmar Gardens with my parents and two younger sisters. My memories of growing up are in the 1950s and the 1960s.

I remember my childhood as a happy, family time. Life was comfortable in a lovely family home with a garden. The house always seemed full of people and as children our friends were always welcome. My sisters and I attended St. Hilary's school. (I never wear purple to this day as the uniform was purple.) We walked to school and back again for lunch and back again for afternoon lessons. My father came home from his office in the West End for lunch every day and I remember him changing his detachable collar before returning to the office.

Lunch on Monday was always cold roast meat, stovies and rice pudding. After school we had a cup of tea while listening to 'Mrs Dale's Diary' – my mother never missed it. We also listened later to Children's Hour.

In summer after school, we played outside if possible. We played tennis and football in Cluny Drive or hopscotch drawn on the pavement. We often climbed a wall beside the coal cellar and got on to the garage roof. Other games included Hide and Seek and Kick the Can. The garden also had a summer house which was used for many imaginative situations. I also remember my father building a model train layout in the garage which we were allowed to play with under his supervision.

In winter there was sledging on Blackford Hill and also down Midmar Gardens into Cluny Drive – I don't know how we turned the corner, thus avoiding the wall. I remember my father skating on Blackford Pond dressed in his tweed plus fours and a flat cap. Although in later years, we always seemed to be trying to get on to the pond when the ice was not thick enough and being chased by the parkie.

Outings included trips to the Zoo, North Berwick and Gullane or across the Forth on the Queensferry ferry.

We went to the King's Theatre to see the 'Five past Eight' show and the 'Fol de Rols'. The best theatre visit was to see 'Peter Pan' but my younger sister was frightened of Captain Hook and was removed screaming from her seat.

We learned to swim and made many visits to Warrender baths and Drumsheugh baths. We were allowed to travel by bus to Warrender baths and often walked home.

Another treat was a matinee performance at the Dominion cinema and walking home, stopping for fish and chips at the shop beside the 'Canny Man' pub.

My sisters and I loved animals and had various cats, budgies and goldfish. However, horses and ponies were the great loves of our lives. I think it began with visits to Cluny Drive of the Hurdy-Gurdy lady; her barrel organ was pulled by a small white pony. I think we were slightly frightened of this small lady dressed in a long skirt but did give her money and tit bits for her pony.

I do remember helping to deliver milk with the Edinburgh & Dumfriesshire Dairy's milk float when they were pulled by horses – the horse was the attraction. What wonderful, patient beasts they were! The electric floats never had the same appeal!

I learned to ride at Spylaw Stables near Colinton and spent many weekends and holidays helping out at the stables in return for free rides. I think I was about 14 years old when we got our own pony Tara, a black mare who we kept in the field at the bottom of Blackford Hill. We used to ride round the Braids and occasionally in the grounds of Charterhall House – although without permission, I suspect.

Holidays were spent in North Berwick. We rented a house for 6 weeks and my father came for a fortnight. Time was spent swimming in the outdoor pool (freezing cold) playing tennis and putting.

I remember the sadness my father in particular felt, at the ending of the trams. My sister and I used to be allowed to go by tram to my father's office in South Charlotte Street for a treat and then have proper afternoon tea in Macvitties tearoom with a choice of cakes from the cakestand on the table.

Another memory is Coronation day in 1953. My parents rented a television set and my mother and her friends watched the whole event sitting in the lounge with their hats on and tea and sandwiches served in my mother's wedding tea service. I remember being incredibly bored with the proceedings and was sent outside to play.

My children and my sisters' children spent many happy days at Midmar Gardens with their grandparents especially feeding the ducks at Blackford Pond, and after my parents died in the 1980s, their grandchildren sponsored a bench at Blackford Pond. We all still go to visit there and the memories come flooding back of happy times.

Characters

Do you remember any particular characters in Morningside?

'The Hurdy-Gurdy lady'

'Yes, the lady used to give you a balloon for rags. I remember she came round. She played the organ but she didn't have a monkey or anything.'

'She took jam jars and things as well as rags if I remember rightly. You were desperate to get anything – a balloon or a goldfish in a thing. She would give you it in lieu of money. I don't think she ever gave out money.'

'Oh no, Oh no.'

'She wanted woollens as well, woollen jumpers.'

'Woollens were prized because they could make up worsted.'

Holidays

What sort of holidays did you have when you were young?

'We went to Caithness. We used to come back home and think the tramcars looked funny because in Caithness they didn't have any. We were away the whole eight weeks holiday.'

How did you travel there?

'Train, it took forever, from about 10 o'clock in the morning till 9 o'clock at night.'

And did you pack trunks and send them on in advance?

'No we didn't but when my girls were young we used to go to Crail and we used to send a trunk on in advance.'

That was a good system. Did the carrier come to the house and pick up the trunk?

'Yes you didn't have to get it down to the station.'

'When we were young we always went away on 1 August and we went by train and the stations – and the trains – were always packed. We didn't go very far, Blairgowrie and places like that, or over to Aberdour. The trunk went in advance because we were a big family.'
Did your parents rent a house or did you stay in a guest house?
'In a guest house, I remember the one over in Aberdour. The boys that were staying there were always keen to bang the gong at meal times.'
And were they allowed to?
'Oh I think so – they'd do it anyway!'

'I went to my grandparents on the Solway in Kirkcudbrightshire and then we always went the last fortnight before we went back to school, to Speyside, to Boat of Garten, I made lots of friends up there. When we went to Galloway – that was by train, and the station was about five or six miles away – my grandfather met us with the pony and trap.'
Where did you get the train to?
'To Southwick station, it was the "Paddy" which was the London Irish train via Stranraer and at Hogmanay it would be passing and you went and listened for them blowing the whistle from the train.'
And that was the sign for the New Year?
'Yes it was.'

'Long ago when my children were very young we took a house over in Fife. We started off in Burntisland where we could stay maybe a month for very little then. We made our own meals and we could do what we liked. Later on, my sister married and had a house in Anstruther and that was a favourite holiday place after that. We found it quite convenient to pop over there by train. We changed at Thornton for Anstruther. We have very happy memories.'
Did you throw pennies into the river when you went over the Forth Bridge? I remember doing that.
'Yes, that's another memory.'
'I didn't go on holiday at all. I lived on a farm 5 miles from Duns

where the nearest station was. If we went to visit our grandmother or aunts we must have walked there and maybe got a bus back. Then there was the Sunday school outing once a year. We joined in with the Duns Sunday school and we went by train then to the seaside places. A lovely day out! That's all I can remember of holidays.'

Sunday school picnics

Tell us a bit about the Sunday school picnics. Do you remember where you went and what you did there?

'New Hailes is the last one I remember. You had your tin – your tinny round your neck.'

'Davidson's Mains was another; do you remember?'

'We had friends who lived in Comiston Road and I'm pretty sure I remember going to see them going on a boat for their Sunday school picnic. I think they were going to Ratho. They would have walked down to Viewforth and got on the boat there and we went up on to the bridge at Ashley and on to the tow path and waved to them as they passed.'

'I think even Colinton Dell was a place we went – a lovely place.'

'We never used to go very far away but it was nice.'

'We went to Dreghorn several times. I don't know if the Army were out there or not but there were fields there. And we went to Roslin and Pinkie House at Musselburgh.'

And it would always be sunny?

'Not at Roslin. We sheltered under part of the ruins of the castle for a while.'

Did you have races – what sort of races?

'Oh yes, egg and spoon, sack races and three-legged races.'

'They still have them don't they?'

'Yes they do.'

'It was fun going on the bus with the streamers, remember the streamers!'

And what did you get to eat?

'You got a bag of stuff – a bag of buns.'

And what did you get to drink in your mug, which you had on a ribbon round your neck?

'Tea, probably tea. Mind you it was a full day's preparation. We

were there for a full day, it wasn't just an afternoon.'
'That's right, we went in the morning. The Superintendent and the teachers set up the races – there were lots of races. And the Church Officer made a fire to boil the urn on for the tea. That was one of the first things that had to be done.'
'They were all quite simple excursions – not elaborate – and the same with our holidays.'

Chapter 2

Domestic life

Perhaps our homes have seen the biggest changes over the last 50 or more years. Here are some of our observations.

Television

Do you remember the Coronation?

'Oh yes, the Coronation, because we all crowded into a neighbour's house to watch it on a 12" black and white telly. During the war, when people used to say, "In America they've got wirelesses that you can see the people on." (Of course we didn't know it was called a television then.) I thought, "I just don't believe that." But we watched the Coronation on this telly, this teeny weeny wee screen and this was just absolutely magic. We were staying in Springvalley. We had a street party between Springvalley Gardens and Springvalley Terrace. There were about 98 of us children, imagine in that area! We had tables out in the street and a small stage, and I think there was a magician and there were two or three that formed a little band and they played. It was the children and the mums and everybody round about. That's the recollection I have of the Coronation, that was June 1953.'

Laundry

When did you have your first washing machine?

'Well my mother never had one, she was never very interested in having a washing machine at all. But it was just a delight for her to have a spin drier.'

'I think I must have been one of the first to have a washing machine. I bought it in 1964 and it was £115. I left my work in 1962 and I got my superannuation money, I think it was £300 and believe you me, that was a fortune! I think I was earning £9 a week when I left so to pay £115 for a washing machine was like 12 weeks wages. I used to keep it in a cupboard and wheeled it out and I had to get garden hoses to stick on the end of the taps because it wasn't plumbed in. My kitchen was kitchen / living room. The kitchen bit just had a cooker.'
'They didn't have fridges – well not many people had fridges.'
'Well I had a fridge and that cost £40 and these figures stick in my mind because it was a lot of money. Gosh! I must have been a whizz with money.'

Before the days of washing machines in the home and laundrettes, many people used laundries for bedding and other large items. Morningside Family Laundry, where the Snooker club is now, was much used, and there was another one, as one of the ladies told us:
'Down the pend in Balcarres Street. After the war they started doing what they called "a bag wash" instead of washing in the tubs.'

But long before that there was another laundry in Springvalley. Tibbie Mackenzie's Granny kept hens in the garden of their large house in Springvalley where the family ran a laundry business. Granny and the hens were a source of great interest to the little girl.

Untitled poem
by Tibbie Mackenzie

My Granny had a day old chick
That wouldnae last the day.
She happt it in a woollen sock
And settled doon to pray.

She tappt it up wi' brandy
And gie'd the bird it neat.
And my did it die happy
Though its life was short and sweet.

Central heating

Another innovation of the late 1950s and early 1960s was central heating. One contributor told of having it installed in her home and of some other home improvements.

'I remember Hepburn the plumber in Comiston Road because they put in our central heating. We were about the first house in the Gardens to have it done and we were sort of guinea pigs because they had never put it in a house before. They were in the whole winter – floorboards up – it was awful but it was working by the early spring. It was a big upheaval but I'm fortunate to have a cellar and the boiler is in the cellar so it's easy to do electrical work or anything.

'Then another thing, you see, all the railings had been taken away [to supply iron for wartime munitions] and those houses were meant to have gates and railings. So we had railings and the main gate and a side gate and double garage gates all done for £75 by the blacksmith in Balcarres Street.

'Other tradesmen I remember: we had Hardie the joiner, also from Balcarres Street, and a shop which is a great miss is Scott the ironmonger. It was a lady who owned it then her nephew took over, and it was the sort of shop where they could find you anything.'

Tenement living

'I lived in Morningside Road at the end of Morningside Park. They were big flats; we had four bedrooms so there were three flats in each stair. When it was your turn for the stair [washing it] this card came round and there was a woman came that did the stair and every so many weeks it was your turn to do the back passage. You paid extra that week and then you passed on the card to the next person. You hung it on the door handle.'

What about the bells at the bottom?

'Well a little man would come and he polished the brass bells at the foot of the stair and that was threepence a week for that. He got threepence from everybody otherwise he didn't polish your bell. Sometimes he would come and do the fanlight over the stair.'

'We used to do the same in Springvalley but the ladies that lived there did it themselves because hardly any of them went out to work in those days when I was young. We didn't have a card; we just knew whose turn it was. But a card came round every sixteen weeks for the back passage. We didn't have fitted carpets in those days, just a wee rug in front of the hearth and little mats at the door of every room. The women came out and brushed their mats at the front stair and polished the bells. It breaks my heart now, to look at these stairs and the bells hanging off. They're neglected.'

Did these flats have electricity or was it all gas?

'We had electricity in Morningside Road.'

'Oh lots of houses in Springvalley had electricity too but you put it in yourself. I was about 12 before we got electric put in the house.'

'It would be about 1949 when we got electricity put into our house. It was a change having had a range with a gas oven and a gas ring. My mother thought life was just so easy once we got an electric cooker and electric light. My father used to say to her – pointing at the range – "That's your God" and she'd say, "What do you mean?" "Well you're aye kneeling in front of it" he would say.'

Other aspects of daily life

'Remember the mangle? My mother used to wash the sheets and put them through the mangle.'

'Another thing my mother used to do; we had a tub, a sink and a bunker and Mother used to fix the mincer to the bunker and I had to sit there to keep it steady while she minced the meat.'

'And when you went to the butcher your mother would say, "Order the steak first and then get them to mince it".'

The talk of washing the stairs and polishing the bells reminded one lady:

'I remember when I was about 10 or so, my mother went to work for a lady who lived in Falcon Road. That lady had a live-in housekeeper and Mum was just the char lady. They had a big hall and they dined in the hall. On school holidays you see, I used to go round with my mother because there was nobody to look after me and I thought this was so unusual, somebody dining in their hall. I thought it just illustrated the difference in the accommodation in Morningside – you know, me in my little room and kitchen in

Springvalley and this lady dining in her hall with a live-in housekeeper and a char lady as well.'

'That's one of the interesting things about Morningside: there is such variety.'

'Does anyone know why we get the reputation for being snobbish in Morningside? They say, "Oh you come from Morningside" in a funny accent and even in the theatre, if you go to the King's Theatre pantomime, they make jokes about living in Morningside.'

'It might be something to do with these enormous big houses round about here. When my father was a postman he went round Hermitage and the cook used to invite him in for breakfast in the morning. He worked from Falcon Road West sorting office. This was a wonderful job because it was well paid and secure and he got a uniform. He used to walk from the Dumbiedykes to Falcon Road West to get the early morning shift – 6 o'clock in the morning or something. Eventually he was offered a house in Comiston Terrace so he didn't have that long walk and then his delivery. My father died when he was 82 and, do you know, he could go up and down stairs and never be out of breath and I'm sure it was all that walking.'

'I used to have a holiday job at Christmas on the Post when I was a student. You were sent to the Falcon Road West sorting office and you were allocated to one of the postmen. He always helped you sort the mail in the morning because he knew the order you should have the streets in and he took you out on the first day to do the walk. After that you were on your own. They were so good, the postmen: they would say things like "Now Mrs So and So will be out so you just go round the back and leave it under the bucket" or "She's got an empty box outside the garage. You just put it in there if she's not in" or "Don't give it to the neighbour, they're not speaking." They were great, they really knew their people.'

'And do you remember the telegraph boys; they came on their bicycles?'

'And when they came you were worried – "Oh a telegram!" These were the days before anyone had a telephone.'

'Usually bad news.'

'Not always, there were greetings ones too with a nice decorated

border round it with the message. They got them at wedding receptions and the telegrams were read out.'
'Now they just send an e-mail. It's not quite the same.'

Shopping

We've talked about going to the butcher for steak and about mail and telegram deliveries. What other shopping and deliveries do you recall?
'I certainly got sent the messages [an old Scottish expression for shopping] quite often when I was really quite young. And do you remember, we used to have a "greengrocer" bag? It wasn't the same bag as you got other things in. You weighed a forpit of potatoes in a boat shaped scale and tipped them into the greengrocer bag and then you weighed the carrots and tipped them in. They were never wrapped. But you didn't use your greengrocer bag to go to the butcher or the baker. So I used to be sent down to get all these dirty vegetables with the greengrocer bag. I do object to all the wrapping nowadays.'
'When you went to the grocer's everything was measured out into paper bags. The sugar was measured out and poured into a blue bag and the flour and so on, from the containers which the Open Door has kept.' [The Open Door in Morningside Road used to be Gillespie's a family grocer.]
'And you went shopping every day because you had no fridge.'
'I can still remember the school holidays, sitting at the kitchen table and my mother saying, "Now you can write out the shopping list -- butter, margarine, something for supper" and off you were sent with the bag and the money.'
The Co-op, generally known as 'the Store' , was a favourite shop for many families. Do you remember the Co-op shops in Morningside Road?
'Where Iceland is now was a Co-op [this was the first supermarket] but the first Co-op I remember where you had the Grocery, was at the corner of Springvalley Gardens where the Bank is. There were wooden shelves and you went in with your ration book and if you were lucky maybe eggs would be in and you would be allowed one or two eggs.'
'And the Bakery was on the other side, where Toys Galore is now. The Butcher was next to the Grocer's and then the Store Chemist was where the coffee shop is.'

'Then there were the Co-op shops in Comiston Road. There was a Grocer there too and a Greengrocer, Baker and Chemist all in the one block.'

'My school chum lived in Comiston Terrace and I used to sometimes chum her to the Store at the corner, and you sat on milk crates while you queued up. It was the same at Springvalley.'

'It was benches we had, we were awful posh. It was the same Store.' [Springvalley]

A memory shared by many:

'I remember when I went to the Co-op for my mother and she had a number and I still remember the number.'

'Do you remember you had a Store book and you handed it in when you got your messages. What was the purpose of that?'

'Well, say your husband was paid at the end of the week, you could get provisions marked into your book then you paid it when your husband gave you some housekeeping money.'

'I remember the Dividend – the Divi – the Store paid out at the end of a term.' That would be calculated from the purchases marked in the book too.'

'Funny how we all talk about the Store and not St Cuthbert's or the Co-op. My brother was telling me a story recently. When he was a boy in Springvalley there was a little shop at the top of Springvalley, Sharp's. A family moved into the street who had just come back from Canada and my brother and some of his pals were standing around when this young boy came walking up Springvalley and they said, "Oh hello, you've just moved in" "Yes," he said, "I'm just going to the store." And they all said, "Oh you're going the wrong way, the Store's up there."

So they both learned something that day, that any shop is called a store in Canada.'

Of course there were all sorts of shops besides the Co-op in Morningside and members of the group recalled some of them with pertinent comments. No doubt readers will remember others.

Grocers

James Rose at Churchill, described as 'a very old fashioned, very Edinburgh grocer'.

Then in Morningside Road there was William Low and, at the corner of Millar Crescent, McLeod where the biscuits were sold loose from large containers in front of the counter and small children were often given one as their mothers were being served. On the other side of Morningside Road, where the Post Office is now, was Templeton's and before that it was Cochrane's.
In Comiston Road were Grossart at the corner of Craiglea Drive, Aitkenhead at the corner of Comiston Drive and Sinclair on the opposite side of Comiston Road.

Bakers
Murray's was the best remembered, famed for its Scotch pies made in their own bakery up the pend and at the back of the shop. One lady told us, 'We had an arrangement with Murray's and we used to go down on a Saturday at 6 o'clock and we used to get a bag of buns for the old sixpence, and we'd have meringues, real cream cookies and iced buns. On Sunday morning my brother and I would make tea for everyone and we'd have it with these lovely buns – a whole bagful for sixpence. What a treat!'
Macvitties Guest in Comiston Road just beyond the school and Young's at the corner of Morningside Drive were also remembered.

Butchers
Dobson at Churchill was mentioned and further down Morningside Road, Meikle and nearer the Station was Waugh.
In Comiston Road there were Leslie's, started in 1928, Hindmarsh, and beside Macvitties Guest there was Stewart Brown.
A group member remembered another butcher who sold 'potted heid'. She remembered it because she did not like it but her family did. She declared it to be disgusting!

Dairies
There were several – Dumfriesshire, Maypole and Buttercup, but the one most often mentioned is the Buttercup, now the Clock Shop in Comiston Road where the Buttercup tiles can still be seen. One contributor remembered watching the butter being patted and the cheese being cut with a wire from the large slabs in the dairy and wishing she could do that.

Fish shops

Fresh fish was a regular part of the family menu and there were many fish shops.

Those best remembered were Bell's ('a nice clean shop'), and Brown's and Main's who had several shops in the area and still have one.

Miss Brown the fishmonger was remembered as being 'a lovely lady' from whom one could buy 'four haddocks for 2s 6d, and tuppenceworth of trimmings for the cat. It was horrible – heads – and you boiled it up at home and fed it to the cat.'

Fish & Chips

Fish is nothing without the chips.

Mention of the Fish & Chip shop next to the Canny Man elicited the comment; 'You look back and think, my conscience, that Fish and Chip shop is still there!'

Many contributors remembered this shop with affection as they did Rossi's ice cream shops.

Sweetie shops

As with dairies, there were numerous sweetie shops, but Miss Lorimer at Churchill was best remembered for her tablet and hand made chocolates with violets on top.

Then another was Lawson's on the south side of the pend at Murray's the baker. It was the tenement above Lawson's that had to be demolished due to subsidence said to be caused by disturbance of the Jordan Burn during the construction of a new BT building in Maxwell Street.

A sweetie shop on the other side of the road was where one of the group remembers dashing over the road to buy a Mars bar the day sweetie rationing finished.

Chemists

Finlay's was remembered as 'the big chemist shop at the corner of Morningside Park' (now Sibbald Travel).

Another chemist remembered was McLennan, a double shop in Comiston Road 'where they had all the big glass bottles in the window and where they mixed the medicines for you.'

Ladies' and men's wear

There were several ladies' wear shops in Morningside, one in Morningside Drive kept by two ladies, where blouses, gloves etc. were purchased. At Churchill, Lena's, Jane Thomson and Avril's were mentioned.

Someone said, 'A lot of us were coming home from school and we said, "when we leave school we're going to buy dresses at Avril's" and that's one of the first things I did: I got a red dress.'

Another told us: 'I was 15 when my brother got married. I got my suit in Avril's for his wedding and I thought I was the bee's knees.'

Yet another remarked: 'When my older daughter was married I got my "mother of the bride" outfit at Avril's. It was lovely.'

On the matter of men's wear:

'I remember there was a gentlemen's outfitter at Morningside Station and for years the shop seemed to be closed. The things just hung in the window getting more and more dusty and cobwebby – it always made me think of Miss Haversham. It was queer, I never remember the shop being open yet it was never emptied of its merchandise.'

Home deliveries

From speaking about shops the group went on to recall deliveries both by van and (especially during the war) by horse.

'Mr Logan came round twice a week with greengroceries and various things. Before that, his grandfather came with a horse and cart when the houses were first built. [Greenbank in the 1930s] Then a baker and a fish man used to come round. It was a great help.'

'The Store van would come round and my mother would give him her list and he would come back with the box of goods, put it on the kitchen table and offer to put it away. The Store also delivered milk.'

'Jimmy Coates the fruit and veg man used to come round.'

'There was a lady lived opposite us, always gave his horse an apple, and if she wasn't out with the apple, the horse was in at the gate with his nose over.'

This sparked off another memory:

'We used to gather the horse droppings for our roses.'
'Yes so did we – out with the shovel!'

Then there was the delivery of coal.
'I can remember my father giving the coalman a cigarette when he had climbed up the stairs with the coal. They had to get it into the house, swing round a couple of doors and tip the coal into the bunker. What a mess! I remember rolling up newspapers and putting them at the base of the doors to keep the dust out of the other rooms. When you think about it now!'
'Living on the ground floor, I was so glad our coal cellar was in the stair, it made such a difference.'

Lack of space has prevented us from recording all the shops remembered by our contributors.

We cannot leave Morningside Road without referring to two other popular landmarks:

The Canny Man
One lady said, 'you get a lovely lunch there'.
Another surprised us when she said, 'My Dad used to say that if you went upstairs on the 23 bus you could look down into the Canny Man and see the Go Go dancers on a Sunday afternoon.'
This elicited the astonished response, 'Really! On a Sunday?'

The Merlin
Another Dad was reported to have said, 'They could just make a door in the back wall and I could walk straight in from Springvalley instead of having to go all the way round.'

Chapter 3

Hospitals and Health

Nurses' homes
'We had one day off a month'

One lady who did her nursing training at Edinburgh Royal Infirmary told us about the Nurses' Home in Canaan Lane.

'I trained at the Infirmary and we were taken there by bus (to Canaan Lane) and we'd all have our red capes on. I used to sneak out because my mother lived in Morningside, and I used to put a pillow in the bed and would have my lunch at home and then sneak back in again.'

So you were not really allowed out?

'Not really, that was your sleeping time because you had a 12-hour nightshift to do. But two or three of my friends used to come along with me, and one of them was a giggler. We were caught going back in one time, because she was giggling.'

And were you disciplined?

'Oh yes. Our late passes were taken – one a year we got, until one in the morning and once every two months you got an 11 o'clock late pass.'

'Goodness! The girls nowadays wouldn't believe that, would they?'

'When I started we had one day off a month.'

'I remember seeing the bus turning out of Canaan Lane, going up to the Royal in the evening and the nurses sitting with their red cloaks and their little white caps on. Oh! I thought you all looked very sophisticated!'

'The Home is part of the Health Education Board now. I used to go back there because I did Occupational Health. It was quite funny going back and remembering.'

Another former nurse's experiences:
'I nursed at the City Hospital and stayed in the Nurses' Home for 18 years. We were sisters and each of us had our own room. I don't know about the nurses, I think they probably did too. The sisters had keys so we could get in and out at any time.'
Were the rules very strict?
'Yes, especially in the Home. We called each other by our last names.'
What was the transport like to get to the hospital?
'Well we had to walk up and down that long avenue. There were no buses running to the hospital then. We walked right out to Comiston road, to the trams. It was pretty bad during the war with the blackout, I believe, because they had all that long way to walk in the dark. Now the 41 bus goes right up – much better. I remember coming back one night after being to see *Psycho*, and I walked in the middle of the road.'

'I had a friend whose father was a gardener at the City Hospital. He liked to tell the story of how one day he was stopped in the grounds by a young man who was looking for the Nurses' Home. The young man wanted to hand in a letter to one of the sisters who he had met at a dance, as he wanted to make a date with her but didn't know how to go about it. So the gardener said, "Well I'll hand it in for you. I know where to take it, but who is it for?" The young lad replied, "Oh I don't know her name, but she is very pretty". So the messenger marched into the Nurses' Home and knocked on a door where the sisters were all sitting in the sitting room and he said "There's a young man asked me to hand in this letter". They all looked interested and one of them asked, "Who is it for?" and he said, "Well you'll have to decide that for yourselves because I can't decide. He just said it was for the pretty one". He said all the nurses jumped up shouting, "It's me! It's me!" '
What sort of social activities did the staff have?
'Not very much, we started a sort of a club when some of us came, (1949) but it fell through after a few years.'

'I believe they had Sports days and a Christmas party for the staff.'
'Oh we had a big Christmas dinner, the Lord Provost used to come and I think there must have been one for the other members of staff. The City Hospital had all their own plumbers, electricians, gardeners and everything.'
'I remember on Christmas Eve the nurses from the City used to come down to Greenbank Church for the midnight service.'
'That's right. We sang carols round the wards first, then went to the dining room for mince pies.'
'You all looked very glamorous in your navy blue capes when you came into church.'
'We always got to sit at the front.'
'Yes, and it was all candlelight.'

Home visits from the doctor

Some memories of childhood diseases; mumps, measles, chickenpox… and more.

'I think the whole time I was at Morningside school I lost one and a half days. I probably had the odd cold but I did not get any illnesses. I was threatened with chickenpox once. The doctor came and he looked at me and he said, "I think it's all over. I think he's missed it. Keep him off school until Monday". So I missed Friday. Another time I had some sort of cough and they thought it was whooping cough, but by the next day it had disappeared so I never got any of these. But we had a boy from Morningside school died of diphtheria during the war. But you never think of it now.'
'My son, he's 29 now, but when he was two he had whooping cough and he was terribly sick. Fortunately we had a nurse across the road and we called her across and she took one look at our son and said, "Oh that's whooping cough," and told us what to do – "Phone the Doctor and tell him I say it's whooping cough and he'll come out in the morning." And he did and he said, "There'll be many a doctor who has never heard that cough and wouldn't know that it was whooping cough". And that was a killer disease.'

One lady said:
'I remember going for my injections, you know for all the

childhood diseases and the doctor saying, "Oh this is the 'Ouch' girl; this is the wee girl who just says, 'Ouch'!" '

'I can remember when I was about five and I got swollen glands, and the doctor – he always came to visit in those days – he bandaged up my head and he did my dolly at the same time. Now, you wouldn't get a doctor doing that today I'm sure.'

'No they wouldn't have time to do that.'

'At that time doctors were on their own in their practices. There were no group practices.'

'Mostly they were on their own and operating from their own house. The surgery was usually a big room, freezing cold, and the waiting room not much better. Perhaps it was to discourage you from going.'

'And it was often the doctor's wife who answered the phone and made the appointments.'

One of our contributors, a retired ENT consultant, had many experiences to share with us.

Were any operations carried out at home?

'Yes, we used to do "Kitchen table tonsils".'

When you went to operate in a house, did you go and scrub up and put your green gown on?

'Oh yes, you brought your own rubber apron with you and you scrubbed up at the kitchen sink. They had kettles of boiling water for you. You brought your instruments ready sterilised, you had them sterilised in the hospital before you came. You brought them to the house, used them, then took them back to the hospital to be cleaned and re-sterilised. You brought an anaesthetist with you. They used mostly ether, or ethyl chloride and ether, at that time with an open mask. You had a frame with a gauze cover and you just dripped the ether on to the open mask and the child inhaled it until the anaesthetist said, "Right, all yours". And you had to get in and out quick.'

Others recalled this mask:

'I can remember being terrified. I could feel this mask going over and I was struggling to fight it. It was a horrible sensation.'

'Yes I did that at the dentist and my mother was black affronted.' To which our surgeon replied comfortingly, "A natural reaction".'

Hospitals and infectious diseases

The retired ENT consultant went on to talk about immunisation. 'Immunisation for diphtheria started about the late 1920s – diphtheria and scarlet fever being the scourge of childhood. Then they were replaced by measles and whooping cough, and even whooping cough was a pretty deadly thing. If you were in the fever hospital, parents were allowed to visit, but you just saw them through the glass while you were still infectious.

'My whole family was in hospital with diphtheria. We were all infected, so we all went in. Mum and Dad got out first, then my sister got home but my brother died in the hospital (he was nine) and I got home after that.'

This sad little story brought back more recollections of children in hospital.

'I knew some people who were in the City Hospital. Anything that went into the hospital with them couldn't come out again, so we used to save up our comics – there were Beanos and Dandies and some others -– and take them in for the children. But we knew they could never come out again, and that meant that if they took their Teddies in they weren't allowed to bring the Teddies out afterwards. But that's going back quite a long way.'

'Going way back, my mother was in the fever hospital with diphtheria when she was four and she was in for about 10 weeks. They used to be taken into the steam room and she was given a penny, an old copper penny, and she was told that if she stayed long enough and behaved well enough in there, and the penny turned green (because it was copper) then she would get to keep it. But if she cried to get out before it turned green then she wasn't allowed to keep it. But that was 90 years ago.'

'My painter told me he had been a patient in the hospital when he was five and he remembered it with sheer horror. It was just as if he had been abandoned completely – and he's almost 60, so that's going back over 50 years. His parents weren't allowed to come and see him and he was in there for about a fortnight without any visitors at all. He thought he was never going to come out again. It was awful.'

Another story confirmed this:

'My brother – probably in the 1930s – got scarlet fever and was taken away and nobody was allowed to go and see him. He used to call it the "Kitty Hospital", and was going to the "Kitty Hospital", and when my mother was allowed eventually to go and see him, he said, "Oh Mummy, I thought you were dead". Because that was the only reason he could think of why she hadn't been to see him.'

'What a shame, how terrible!'

'The parents used to go and stand outside the windows in the grounds and wave to the children. I used to see these little kids standing at the windows, it meant so much to them just to be able to wave to their mummies. There would be quite a lot of parents because it was a big hospital and they were coming from quite a long distance.'

'Do you remember the bulletins they used to publish in the *Evening News,* with the patients' numbers?'

'It said, "Dangerously ill, family requested to come out", and there would be a wee list of numbers. And then, "Seriously ill, no immediate danger", and another wee list of numbers. Then, "Satisfactory", and more numbers. I can't remember all the categories.'

'Fortunately, "Satisfactory progress" was the biggest list.'

'Of course people didn't have phones in those days, and that's how they found out their child's progress – or otherwise.'

One group member who worked at the City Hospital from 1949 until retirement in 1981, was a sister on the TB wards.

'We had about six or eight TB wards, male and female. A few years after I went there they opened a theatre so they could do all these terrible operations the poor people had to go through, you know, collapsing their chest wall, removing ribs and all that kind of thing. They don't do that nowadays though, they depend on drugs. Professor (now Sir) John Crofton pioneered the drug treatment. From the original eight TB wards in the beginning, there were only seven male patients left when I retired.'

Was that because TB was being eradicated?

'Because the drugs were so efficient. TB was a killer before that. I had one admission book from earlier years and the deaths were written in red and every page had RED, RED, RED – and they were all young, just 16 to 21 years old.'

'There was a whole ward of children with TB at the Princess Margaret Rose Hospital for many years.'

'That was because they were spinal, they wouldn't be infectious.'

'I remember the beds out in the open on the verandas at the Princess Margaret Rose Hospital.'

'Oh yes, that was always the cure – fresh air.'

[The Princess Margaret Rose Hospital was opened in 1930 as a hospital for children.]

'What strides they have made in the treatment of TB!'

'Yes, one young man with spinal TB had a bone graft done and had a kidney and a lung removed as well. When he was discharged eventually, he worked as a lion keeper at the zoo, feeding the lions. I'll always remember him, six years we had him.'

'Then there were all the other infectious diseases; we had two patients in the iron lung. They stayed in there sometimes for years, until they died, poor things, they were never cured. Polio was a terrible scourge. They had to lie flat on their back – they were paralyzed – and the iron lung breathed for them, They couldn't live outside of it.'

Another group member had been told of the smallpox epidemic during the war.

'Patients were isolated in a special hut and nurses were asked to volunteer to work there. One of the porters volunteered to work there too. He used to watch for one of the gardeners on his way home, give him some money and ask him to get him some cigarettes. The gardener was quite happy to do this. But when he mentioned it at home his wife said, "You shouldn't be doing that. That man is in there with all these smallpox patients and handing you money". And the gardener realized he had been going home to his wife and two young children and he might have been taking smallpox with him.'

Our nursing Sister added,

'Yes, we were not allowed to go out in our uniform (because of the risk of carrying infection). However it had huge grounds you know, the City Hospital, and you could go for a long walk.'

'The grounds were well cultivated and a team of gardeners worked there growing flowers and vegetables for the hospital. A gardener told me how they used to dig up fresh vegetables; cabbages, carrots, rhubarb or whatever, and deliver them to the kitchen in a wheelbarrow every morning, depending on what the chef had ordered. Of course the City Hospital has gone now and in its place is a housing complex called Greenbank Village.'
One lady summed it up thus:
'This reminds me of when I was a wee girl and we used to go up Fairmilehead way and I used to get fed up with my mother saying, "I mind when this was all fields." Gosh! I can say it myself now, "I mind when this was a hospital, not all these houses".'

Another contributor reminded us that not all tonsils and adenoids were removed on the kitchen table.
'I was "done" at the Sick Children's Hospital. I went up in the morning, had my tonsils out and I got home that afternoon. That's the way they used to do it, you know. A cot was shared with two kids, one at each end, and provided you had stopped bleeding by tea time, you got to go home.'
'And they told you you'd get ice cream.'
'That's right.'

Another contributor recorded her voluntary work at the Royal Edinburgh Hospital.
'I did the canteen along there three afternoons a week in a ward kitchen. Later we moved to a ward with a veranda, hence the name "The Veranda Tearoom", now operating every day, morning and afternoon. We also ran rehabilitation groups, meeting occasionally for meringues and tea, and playing games with the patients. It was a bit of befriending at that time and patients came down from the wards. Then we ran a sewing group, mending things for the patients to save money. But that stopped because the paid staff who used to do a bit, objected that we were doing it for nothing.'
'That was a pity because it was therapy, you were involving the patients.'

Recollections of well-known surgeons and consultants

'We had lock-up garages in Comiston Terrace and one interesting gentleman who kept his car there was R. I. Stirling – he lived in Cluny Drive.'

Was he a surgeon?

'I associate him with the PMR [Princess Margaret Rose Hospital].'

'He had a wonderful knowledge of Skye and all its folklore. I used to keep the garage open until midnight to get all the cars parked away and the Doc (that was his other name) used to come in about 11.30 pm after finishing his last nursing home. Out would come his pipe and he would sit down in the office and the stories he would tell! They were wonderful. One of the things R. I. Stirling specialised in was brain injuries, head injuries from mine accidents in Fife. And they would hold the ferry for him when they knew he was going over to Kirkcaldy and the ferry men would always wait for him for the last ferry on the way back. He always used to time a journey in pipes – Inverness was a four-pipe trip, and he would have four pipes lined up along the dashboard. We were overhauling the engine of the Doctor's car at one time and we took it to the chap who did our engine re-boring. And when we said it was a surgeon's car, and we needed it back as soon as possible, he asked, "Who is it?" and when he was told, R I Stirling, he said, "Right, it will be done tomorrow, and there will be no charge. He saved my life ten years ago, so anything you want for him – no charge." He was a wonderful man. But it was unfortunate, he retired and then got bone cancer, and George Pollock, who took over from him at PMR, had to operate. He took his leg off at the knee and that didn't work so he took it off at the hip. But R. I. Stirling was so well thought of that the Russians sent over an artificial leg for him. They were world leaders in prostheses.'

Recollections of some other well-known Edinburgh Consultants of the late 1940s:

'I studied Medicine at Edinburgh Medical School commencing in 1939 and after graduating I did six months in hospital to get my clinical training. That was at Edinburgh Royal Infirmary.

'There would be 30 patients in a ward. First thing in the morning, nine or before, you went round with the ward sister. You got everything ready and the Consultant didn't arrive till 10 am. You were supposed to have everything done before he came.'

Who were some of the well-known Consultants then?

'Surgery was Sir John Fraser, medicine was Stanley Davidson, then Sir John Bruce was a general surgeon. Then in my own line, ENT, there was Simpson Hall and Ewart Martin and Charlie Scott was with the Sick Kids. Professor Norman Dott was there at that time, he was up in ward 20. Walter Mercer was the orthopaedic surgeon, I did part of my surgical training with him. One of the other surgeons was Frankie Jardine. Then after my clinical training I went into the army and had three years out in the Middle East.'

Nursing Certificate

One lady whose aunt had trained at the City Hospital in its early days brought along her certificate. The document was parchment:

'Nurse Anne Donald entered the City Hospital on 15th April 1907 and has undergone in its wards three years training in the practical work of fever nursing. Also she has had the benefit of systematic instruction by lectures and classes and is, in our opinion, a qualified fever nurse, competent to undertake the nursing of infectious diseases.'

The certificate was signed by:
A. Maxwell Williamson, Medical Officer of Health
Claude B. Kerr, Medical Superintendent
I. Thomas, Matron
Approved by Public Health Committee
John McPherson Convener, Edinburgh July 15, 1910

This reminded someone in the group that, in his book about the City Hospital, Dr James Gray mentions that, in the early years of the hospital, some of the young nurses fell victim themselves to these dreadful infectious diseases. Their names were recorded in the Matron's log book, first as admissions to a ward, and subsequently as deaths.

Deaths and burials

It seems appropriate to include here an item contributed by the daughter of a former Superintendent of Morningside Cemetery.
'My father was the Superintendent at Morningside Cemetery and the house where we stayed was just where you entered the cemetery at Belhaven. The cemetery was owned and run by Metropolitan Cemeteries and the graves, paths, Superintendent's house and gardens were all beautifully kept – mark you, my father had a staff of 11 working under him. Like most homes, the house had no electricity, just gas, and you had to run your radio off batteries. Behind the house was a source of water for anyone putting flowers on graves and a bin for the disposal of dead flowers. It is a measure of how much attention was paid to individual graves that a horse and cart were used to take the flowers to the tip at the west end of the cemetery where the flats are now. There was an extensive range of glasshouses and cold frames at the back of the house facing Balcarres Street, which were used to keep the cemetery supplied with bedding plants. The horse was black and called Pongo. In those days the cemetery was regarded as a suitable place to walk particularly on a Sunday. People wishing to visit the cemetery after 6 p.m. when the gates were closed could get a key for the small gate for £1. My sister and I had great freedom and the run of the gardens and cemetery once the gates were closed. We were never really put-out by living within the cemetery walls, though in later years, we had to carry a key for the big gates when we went out in the evening, and we didn't hang about getting into the house. A common comment was that we lived in the "dead centre of Morningside" and my father was known to say that "we were never bothered by our neighbours". The cost of upkeep of most graves was charged on an annual basis – the four of us would have to write out the 2000 accounts annually, though some were funded in perpetuity. Although the cemetery contains graves from the First World War, I cannot bring to mind any specific military funerals.'
This item reminded another lady:
'I can recollect my mother saying that at the time of the influenza epidemic in 1918–1919, on one day ten little white children's coffins passed by along Caanan Lane on the way to the cemetery.'

Children's choir/concert, Morningside Parish Church, early 1950s (Photograph: Marjory Paul)

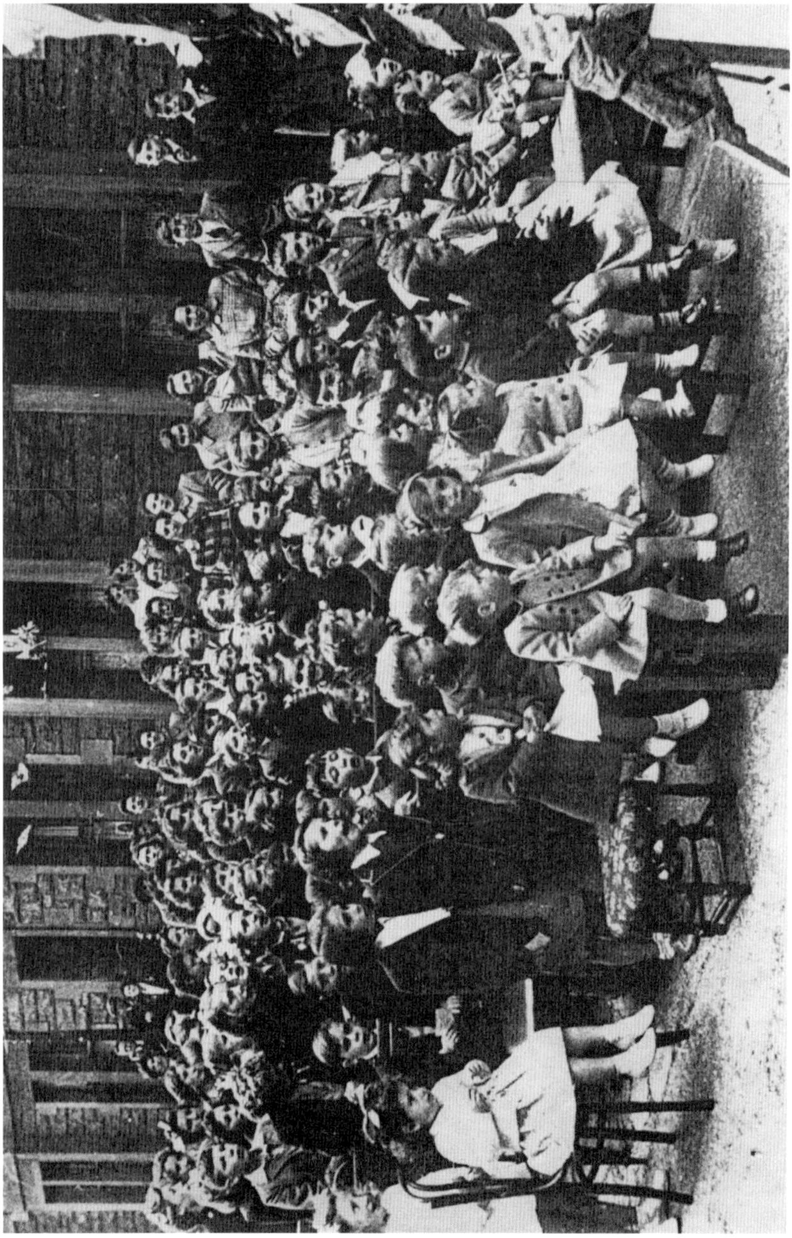

Coronation street party on 2 June 1953 in Millar Place (Courtesy of W. Ovens)

Coronation street party on 2 June 1953 in Millar Place
(Courtesy of W. Ovens)

Guide's outing, Morningside Parish Church
(Photograph: Marjory Paul)

Main's Fish delivery van, probably at Greenbank, in June 1936
(Courtesy of Malcolm Cant Publications)

Steel's Place, either on a Sunday or a Wednesday early closing day!
(Courtesy of Malcolm Cant Publications)

Superintendant's house, Morningside Cemetery (Courtesy of Margaret McGregor)

Morningside Cemetery workers in the 1930s (Courtesy of Margaret McGregor)

Centenary of South Morningside School: Mrs Elizabeth Notman, the oldest surviving former pupil, cutting the cake (Photograph: Marjory Paul)

The Canny Man's on the corner of Morningside Road and Canaan Lane in 1987 (Photograph by Phyllis M. Cant)

The Dominion Cinema in Newbattle Terrace when there were only two screens (Photograph by Phyllis M. Cant)

Morningside Station looking north with the clock in its central position, 1987 (Photograph by Phyllis M. Cant)

Kay's Bookshop in Morningside Road, 1987 (Photograph by Phyllis M. Cant)

Chapter 4

Entertainment

Dance halls

'Oh how we danced'...at the Silver Slipper, the Plaza, the Abbotsford and the Assembly Rooms.

Safeway used to be Jones Motor House and the Plaza Ballroom. Did you go to the Plaza when you were girls?
'Oh yes, and the Silver Slipper in Springvalley Gardens.'
'I believe it had a very nice floor.'
'Yes, very nice but not very large.'
'I remember going for tap dancing lessons at the Silver Slipper.'
'Oh yes, Madam Ada, she certainly took classes in the area because girls in my class went to Madam Ada for dancing.'
'Then Jean Reynolds was for Highland dancing.'
'I remember the Silver Slipper but I never attended it. My Mother said that it was only bad women who went to the Silver Slipper!' [This remark was greeted with much laughter and cries of protest from the others present.]

'I remember the Plaza. Our second meeting was at the Plaza. In fact, my husband (then boyfriend) had an uncle who played in the dance band; he was the one who led it. In the Plaza there used to be two dance halls. There was the big one where you went if you were, kind of, on your own and it was sort of the meeting place. And then (having got a partner), it was a case of "Would you like to go down to the small hall?" And you passed through the cafe where you got offered coffee – absolutely no alcohol! Over coffee you decided whether you were going to go back up to the big hall (to find a better partner) or whether you were going to go into the small hall which was where my husband's uncle had his dance band. Of course once I went down to the small hall with him it was virtually a commitment because his uncle was there, winking and nodding! So yes, the Plaza was very much a popular place for us to go. The other thing I remember about going to the Plaza in the 1960s was we all wore – the girls all wore – these very full skirted dresses and we used to fold our big net underskirts up, push them down a stocking or something so that we could carry them in; you couldn't wear them under your coat. So it was quite amusing, seeing in the ladies'cloakroom, all the girls trying to slip their big hoopy underskirts under their dresses. Taking them home after was more awkward especially if you had just met someone and he was seeing you home and he would say, "What's that?" '

'I had a friend on the phone the other day and we were reminiscing about the Plaza and how you could only go to the small hall if you had a partner, and the days when it was teas and soft drinks and you went home with complete strangers and you didn't think twice about it, and nothing happened to you.'
What dances were popular at that time? [1940s]
'Well it was the waltz, the quickstep, the slow foxtrot – things like that. They didn't have any Latin American. These were mostly the dances in the 1940s. The boys were at one side and the girls at the other side; very much separated. The boys had to cross the floor to take a partner and you either wished it was you, or didn't, depending on who he was! There was a band and a singer as well, a girl singing. We used to go downstairs and have a cup of tea. It finished at 11pm and then we came home.'
'On Friday and Saturday it was Late Night (at the Plaza). It finished at one in the morning and we used to walk up to Greenbank. Two of us, and no worries at all. Changed days!'
What were the popular dance tunes and bands? Do you remember?
'Tunes, I can't remember. Dan Delaney was the dance band that was at the Plaza. There was always a big queue away down Morningside Road on Friday and Saturday night.'
'There were other dance halls as well as the Silver Slipper in

Springvalley and the Plaza. Further down there was somewhere you went to learn to dance. Was it called the Abbotsford?'

'Oh yes, just behind the Baptist Church.'

'My husband went there just out of curiosity the other day as he was walking past, because we used to go there. He walked up just to reminisce about his dancing days at the Abbotsford. It is all modern flats now. He just discovered that.'

'There was a hotel along Nile Grove and they used to have a country dance in the conservatory bit at the end. We used to go along there when it was a hotel but it has been a few things since then.'

Did you have live music or was it records?

'I think it was records. It was just the people in the hotel who were running it and it was a smallish hotel. It was the Johnstones, I remember. They had five children so possibly that was to help entertain them.'

Did any of you go to big dances or balls in the Assembly Rooms in George Street? A lot of firms had their Christmas dances there.

'Well I remember going to some of the Caithness Society dances there and when you came out you got a mug of soup at one in the morning. It was great!'

And what did you wear?

'Long dresses, oh, long dresses, you got dressed up.'

And what did the gentlemen wear?

'Oh, evening dress.'

And gloves?

'Not so much, the ladies wore gloves.'

Who did the catering? Did they have caterers in – Macvitties or Crawfords?

'I think it was R. T. Gibson. It was a running buffet, you could go back again and again.'

Was the buffet in the downstairs hall, and the dancing upstairs in the one with the chandeliers?

'Yes, that's right.'

That would be lovely! And what sort of dances did you do – Scottish country dancing or purely ballroom?

'It was mainly ballroom dancing, but they did have an eightsome reel usually, and some strathspeys and other reels.'

A lot of people have spoken about going dancing at the Plaza but not so much about parties there. Were there parties?
'Oh yes, if anyone was having a party at the Plaza it was very upmarket. One which I was taken to – you know Dainty Dinah – well they were what Cadbury's is today – well, Dainty Dinah always had a party for their staff's children and I was always allowed to go. And wedding receptions were often in the Plaza as there was nowhere else locally. It was rather nice because you had the main ballroom and the guests would sit in the balcony and be taken down to dance.'
'Wedding receptions in the Plaza were quite something! It was the place to go in those days.'
'I went to many parties in the Plaza. You had your fun and games – your Looby Loos and whatnot upstairs in the ballroom and then you went downstairs for tea. Then I can remember during the war there was a big ball for the Red Cross and my mother said, "You get some of your friends around and we'll call this your 21st birthday party." So my 21st birthday party was held in the Plaza along with the hundreds and hundreds of Red Cross ticket holders!'
'The other place that was quite popular for parties was Abbotsford Lodge. You went up the little pathway between the Baptist church and – I can't remember what the corner shop was.'
'The Scotsman.'
'It was! I tried to remember not so long ago what used to be there; later it was Hook, Line and Sinker. Well you went up there on the cobbles and you turned left and there were one or two houses up there and then the big garden and then Abbotsford itself. That's where a lot of parties were.'

Cinemas

'Two for the 1s 9d's . . . Those were the days!'

Did you go to the cinema a lot? Was the Dominion a favourite?
'Oh yes, the Dominion.'
'You queued down the side.'
'It was different seat prices –1s 6d, 1s 9d, and I don't know – was it 2s?'

'And 9d half price.'
'Oh yes!'
'And Mr Cameron used to come out and say, "Two for the 1s 9d's", or "I'm expecting a big lift any minute so it is worth waiting." Then, you could sit all day in the cinema.'
'Yes, wasn't it funny how we would quite happily see the last bit of a film, watch the news and the adverts then watch the film round again having seen the denouement.'
'That's probably why they never really knew how many people were coming out!'
'And if you sat to the very, very end you had to sit through the National Anthem.'
'Stand! Stand for the National Anthem. People used to make a hasty exit going, "Quick, quick, before it started."'
Do you remember the Royal wedding in 1947?
'We couldn't have seen it on television, it must have been Pathe News in the cinema.'
'Yes, it was great when you went to the cinema to get the news from all around the world.'
'But the wedding, that wasn't in Technicolour. I think the wedding was in black and white.'
'Yes, I'm sure, because I think Pathe News was always in black and white. When we used to go to the cinema, I just remember nudging people and saying, "Oh it's in Technicolour, this one." I can't remember any colour at Princess Elizabeth's wedding.'
'I think we are very lucky with the Dominion Cinema. It is different than what it was 20, 30 years ago.'
'It has moved with the times though, and kept going because of that.'
'But it is still a family cinema and there's always plenty films that you could take young people to, or your mother to – it is very family orientated.'
'But everyone eats all the time now – that's a sore point with me.'
'Yes, all that crunching from behind!'

Another of the group told us:
'We used to go to the cinema in Springvalley Gardens and they used to advertise a film, but when you went in you were asked

what film you wanted and so many said this, and so many said that, so they just put something on whether you wanted it or not. I don't remember when it closed down, but after that it became the Silver Slipper dance hall.'
[The cinema closed in 1938, just after the Dominion opened.]

Prelude to Saturday Matinee
by Tibbie Mackenzie

Brash hurdy-gurdy, loud and staccato,
Setting the pace to our Saturday feet
As we march with our threepences pocketed safely
To Springvalley Cinema's once a week treat.

Neat wee Italian, somebody's granny,
Cawin' the handle, tapping her toe,
Topknot askew in the Morningside mistral
That's blowing blue murder, threatening snow.

Bold Shetland pony, eyelashes flashing,
Shaking its mane to ward off the sleet.
'It's looking at you,' my brother says blandly.
I dig in my pocket and part with a sweet.

One of the men in the group told us:
'I have in my possession an *Evening News* of 1951 and there were 50 picture houses and about 30 dance halls listed in the front of the News. I took the paper along to my golf club and we had a member there and he reckoned he could name the lot and he almost did. He got about 47 out of 50 cinemas which was marvellous. He was picturing Edinburgh, going along Princes Street – they used to have three or four places in Princes Street – and then you went down Leith Walk and there was this and that – the La Scala and the Alhambra.'
'It was very much your local cinema you went to, now you get in the car and go somewhere else.'

Theatre

'Now you'll know what I'm talking about when I say "the Gods"...'

'We used to go to the theatres a lot: repertory companies Wilson Barrett and Brandon Thomas at the Lyceum. And of course, the King's Theatre – it was 6d for "the Gods". Now, you'll know what I'm talking about when I say "the Gods". There was the Upper Circle, but I remember sitting above that, up all these flights of stairs, and it was awful, padded concrete seats.'

'And that awful view down to the front!'

'And there was no handrail.'

'I remember a friend and I went to the King's Theatre one time, it must have been during or just after the war. It was something we both very much wanted to see and I didn't dare tell my mother how much it was. We went in the 8s seats, I think it was the Grand Circle.'

And what was the show?

'You know, I can't remember!'

'I remember being taken to Peter Pan with the Brownies, at the King's Theatre. I was absolutely thrilled watching them flying and then my sister and my cousin and I played at trying to fly, jumping off a chest of drawers in the bedroom.'

Did it work?

'No – and we were soon stopped.'

'My mother took my sister and the next door neighbour took her daughter to the pantomime, (obviously I wasn't old enough) and the two little girls spent the afternoon playing houses under the seats. Another time when they were taken and had seats in a box, my sister and her friend – who can't have been more than five and seven – insisted on sitting on the top with their legs dangling over! I think that put my mother off the theatre. But we were always taken to Gilbert and Sullivan and you dressed up.'

'Oh you dressed up until just a few years ago if you were going to the theatre.'

'Oh yes, that was part of the fun.'

What sort of dresses did you wear for that?

'Oh you wore your party frock.'

What sort of material would it be: velvet or taffeta or…?
'If it was the winter it would be velvet probably and little pumps.'
'Dancing pumps yes, but I don't think it was ever velvet, it would be taffeta, that was the great thing. I can remember one that was taffeta underneath and a bit of net on top.'
Were they bought or did your mother make them?
'My mother was a good dressmaker; she also made fancy dresses. I remember being a strawberry one time, and I've still got the photograph – not of me as a strawberry, but of my little brother as a strawberry. So it must have been passed down.'
Do you remember when the Braidburn Valley had a theatre?
'Oh yes, it was always very good. You used to take your cushions with you (to sit on the grass steps).'
'It was good, but climatically not so good.'
'I saw a Shakespeare play there, I think it was "As you like it".'
'I remember going to a Dog Show there.'
'Yes, that was a regular.'
'Someone told us that they could remember in one of the productions, a boat cruising down.'
'What was the show?'
'It was "Merrie England", and Queen Elizabeth arrived by boat on to the stage.'
'It was lovely, beautifully done.'
'I wouldn't have thought there would have been enough water to have a boat.'
'It was dammed, the burn was dammed further up and the boat came down in front of the auditorium.'
'I'm laughing because if we have any more rain like the last two days, we'll be having liners on the Braid Burn.'
Were the actors and actresses professionals or amateurs?
'Oh amateurs, they were all amateurs. I think it was the Southern Light Opera Company.' [See the note at the end of this section.]
When would that be?
'In the late 1940s.'
'Something I never remember is sitting in the rain. Perhaps we didn't go if it was raining.'
'It never seemed to rain.'
'No, but I expect it did.'

'We played in the Braidburn Valley a lot, but there was an unwritten rule that you never went on the stage area. Funny how we observed that rule!'
[The Southern Light Opera Company did two productions in the Braidburn Valley open-air theatre. The week beginning 3 June 1946 they produced "Merrie England" which was the first amateur opera to be produced in this theatre, apparently on the lines of a pageant using the whole area as a stage. The Parks Department supplied a profusion of shrubs and flowers to dress the stage, and also the burn was dammed to give sufficient depth for Queen Elizabeth to make her triumphal entry by royal barge.
The weather was not too kind, and the Wednesday performance was cancelled due to severe gales.
In June 1947 they produced "The Vagabond King" and again the weather caused havoc. The Tuesday evening performance was interrupted by a gale blowing and wrecking the custom built scenery. Not surprisingly, no further outdoors performances were put on by the Company.]

Interview with Mr Derek Cameron, owner of the Dominion Cinema

Can you tell us a bit about the history of the cinema?
'My father built the cinema and we opened the doors on 31 January 1938. My first formative memory is having a glass of juice on the day. I remember it quite distinctly because I spilled the juice and thought I was going to be in trouble, but my father just came up, wiped it up, gave me another juice and that was it! Then, all my years of school, if my mother was out or something like that, I would come in here, probably about 4 o'clock and my father would say, "Well, I'll run you home at teatime." He would always give me something to do so I was checking tickets in the front hall when I was seven. During the holidays, he would give me a brush and say, "Go and paint under the seats." There was no carpet, just concrete. That was my holiday job. I was always covered with black gloss paint. My father died in 1948 when I was 12, so I still had a few years at school. My mother carried the cinema on over that time. She did it very astutely and cleverly because when everyone else was starting to play X-certificate films she refused. People always knew they wouldn't be shocked or horrified if they came to the Dominion. It was only when I twinned the cinema in 1972 that we expanded our horizons and played something that maybe wasn't quite suitable for the Dominion! But this was a good thing because we attracted a bigger audience.

'When I came into the business in 1954, there were 35 cinemas in Edinburgh – all functioning. In the 1950s, of course, television appeared, so we immediately thought, "How do we counteract that?" And that's when the cinema industry went into colour. But television closed a lot of cinemas because people were looking for a more comfortable night out. If cinemas hadn't put carpets down or didn't have heating on then they went to the wall.

'The next phase was when television got colour, so what could we do then? We went on to a thing called "wide screen". People could see colour in their own home, but they came to the cinema to see this colossal screen. That was just towards the end of the 1950s into the 1960s. But the architectural design of the building had to be such that it could accommodate this large screen. A lot of cinemas couldn't cope with that, so another batch closed. Then in the 1980s, the video market started. We did think at one point, "This is going to be bad for us." But it was actually like having a trailer. People who saw films on video said, "Oh, I wish I had seen that in the cinema," so we were able to combat that quite successfully.

'So here we are, right up to the present day. We then had to increase the number of screens in the theatre to give people a bigger choice. In 1972 we twinned, in 1980 we put in another one, and just in the 1990s, we've put in another one; so we've now got four cinemas. Now all these multiplexes are opening in the city, but we are very fortunate to have a very loyal band of people who just like coming to the Dom! They always get a "good evening" or a "good night". That's our saving grace, that we have this personal attention and I think a lot of people value that.'

You said that the cinema opened in 1938. Can you tell me why your father picked this site, or what was here before that?

'Yes, well it is quite interesting. It was in 1972 that we discovered that it had originally been a quarry. When we cut down quite a number of feet looking for extra support for our new floor for the twin cinema, we came across a quarry that had been worked. You could see where the chisels had been going into the stone. I don't think it was any special stone, so it had been filled up and was a market garden. So when my father found the site, he bought a market garden. It belonged to the Merchant Company. He managed to purchase the land (which is now flats) running down towards Safeway. The land lay for years as an open space, and I wish I had turned it into a car park! He then bought all of Falcon and set up the Falcon Housing Company. They built all the Falcon houses. He was so determined not to have another cinema – he made it all houses. I have a box upstairs with all the Falcon papers listing the original owners of all the houses and what they paid, in beautifully bound books. It's fascinating. He also bought land up at Buckstone – and that was the Buckstone Housing Company.

'The gentleman who had the Springvalley Cinema was a great friend of my father and he said, "Well, Willie, when you open I'll be closing. I'm going to turn it into a dance hall," which he did.

Just two weeks after the Dominion opened, he closed his doors. If you go in there now – it's the Pine Furniture Store – you'll see it's the same terrazzo, the same steps as here at the Dominion. My father looked at those and said, "Oh, these are good looking steps." He copied that from the Springvalley Cinema. So that's quite interesting.'

There have been great changes in the way the cinema runs. Do you remember the days when it was a continuous programme?
'Yes! Isn't it incredible that people came in halfway through the feature and sat round happily until the time they came in? We were the first people to play a film for a week, instead of just three days, with a film called *Inn of the Sixth Happiness*. We thought we'd try it and we were absolutely mobbed. Now, I know that that film would have done about 15 weeks' business. And we were the first people to have separate performances. Because *Inn of the Sixth Happiness* was such a big film, we made an occasion of it and said, "You'll have an afternoon performance, a middle performance and an evening performance." It worked beautifully. That would have been in the 1950s, when television started. People would watch television Monday, Tuesday, Wednesday and then go to the cinema either Thursday, Friday or Saturday; it gave them a choice.'

And did you still have a second film and a newsreel and cartoons?
'We still had a B-movie and a newsreel, but the newsreel really collapsed after the start of television, so we said, "Forget the newsreel". Then we went into a thing called, "Look at Life", but that became a boring adjunct and people began to say, "We can't be bothered with these B-movies and the adverts" and started coming in just for the feature film and we used to give them a cartoon. But slowly, it got down to just one feature film and the adverts. Now people sit and watch the adverts as if it's the B-movie!
'The Dominion was the first cinema in Edinburgh to have a non-smoking policy. When I opened the Cinema 3 I said, "Cinema 3 will be a no-smoking cinema." All the cinema managers got together and decided that if we all adopted a non-smoking policy then nobody would be able to score a march on anybody else. So

we all stopped the same week and we said, "No smoking in any of the auditoriums." It has been absolutely marvellous from the point of view of the décor and the building. We still have a small section just off the bar in the cinema for people still to have a puff, but that's it.'

I'm trying to recall some of the early films I saw here because this would be the first cinema I was brought to. I remember 'Snow White'.
'Well, it was made in 1938 and, after we opened in January 1938, we played it at Easter. In those days, when the witch appeared there would be a mass exodus of children on the pretext of going to the toilet. Then they would creep back and you would see them look through the doors to make sure there was nothing frightening on. Now the children sit through things like that, totally blasé. There's nothing frightens them at all now, quite unmoved. The last time we played *Snow White and the Seven Dwarfs,* probably about four or five years ago, not a soul moved.'

Another film I remember must have been one of Elizabeth Taylor's earliest films, 'National Velvet'. Elizabeth Taylor played the part of the young girl, didn't she?
'Oh yes. She was a real crowd puller. Clark Gable, Spencer Tracey, Merle Oberon, Lana Turner, Ava Gardner, any of those people could fill the cinema.'

Does that apply today?
'It still applies to a certain extent. Sean Connery can still fill the cinema and Billy Connelly. I mean, *Mrs Brown* was a very successful film. People like Judi Dench of course can also pull in the crowds because people know they are going to get value for their money. All the Dames we've got now can still pull the people in. Quite a number of actors, Brad Pitt and Jude Law for example, are the very latest addition to the glamour boys; the girls will come to see them quite happily. So there's still star value but nothing on the same standing as Barbara Stanwyck and Clark Gable. People would be fighting to get in to see them. And the happy days with Laurel & Hardy, B-movies again, but you just had to put a Laurel & Hardy on and the people rushed to see

them.

'Until the start of the Second World War, we had always been relying on America for films, and then the British films started to come out suddenly. *The Hasty Heart, Above the Waves*: all these wonderful patriotic films – and they did exceptionally well. But there was always space left on the supply ships coming over from America for the American films to come across here. Do you remember Dagwood Bumpstead and Blondie? They never got tired of him and old Gabbie Hayes in the Westerns; he always had the same part.

'And of course, we didn't open on Sundays for years until people said, "Why are you not open on a Sunday?" They just didn't understand I was here by myself at that time and it was my only day off. However, having brought two sons and a daughter into the business now, I am able to say, "Ok, I'm not doing Sunday, but if you want to do Sunday, you split it between you." That's how we are now open on Sundays.'

And of course, you take telephone bookings?

'Oh yes, we've moved with the times, but we've now got in the advert "You're speaking to real people." We don't just have a message like all the rest do.'

You mentioned the value of the personal touch. I think that is something people always comment on about the Dominion – being greeted and so on. People do appreciate that.

'Yes, this is what we really try for; we don't take people for granted. We try to give them a good night's entertainment in comfortable, warm surroundings, and that's what we strive for. We are quite happy to hear any comments on the way out.'

You have very nice catering facilities. When did you start that?

'We've been doing that since 1968. All I was ever going to do was coffee, biscuits and tea. But people were saying, "Can I not get a bacon roll or something savoury?" So I bought a griddle grill and then somebody said, "Can I not get chips?" It was then that I put in a full range – fish & chips, scampi & chips, etc. As time went on, we realised we were going to have to replace the equipment and then Mrs Grant, our cook, a super lady, was retiring and I thought, "When she goes we are not going to have the same standard of cooking." So we stopped the whole thing and incorporated the bar and called it a café / bar and offered healthy options: baguettes, baked potatoes with various fillings, a very simple operation. Where the restaurant was we turned that into a cinema and got back to our core business.'

How many people do you employ in the cinema?
'We have 48 altogether. A lot of them are part-time. We have three full-time projectionists and because everything is automated, one man can look after four projection rooms by himself. He just starts the film and everything is automated, so with three men we can manage quite nicely. Our cashiers, the box office staff, are permanent and everybody else is just part-time, which works very well.'

And you are into third generation family?
'Yes, third generation family running the business. I've now got five grandchildren, which is rather nice. I hope one of them will come in eventually. It would be very nice if they did.'

Do they come into the cinema?
'Oh yes, they are all cinemagoers.'

Was there an upstairs in the original cinema?
'Oh yes, we had a front circle, the back balcony, the back stalls and the front stalls. I've still got the existing boards. During the war, there was a special unit of the Home Guard used to come in and disappear down into our basement. It was only in 1972, when I was making all the changes, that we threw out about 100 helmets and gas mask cases. All the rubber was perished, but they were Army gas mask cases, it was obviously a stock. Further along Newbattle Terrace you know, at Number 11, there was an underground BBC studio, so I don't know if this was to guard it, I've no idea.'

When did you stop playing the National anthem?
"Well, we were having friction. There were people who stood to

attention and others who didn't bother, so all the managers went to the City and they said, "You have to play it at the start of the day." So we played it at the start of the day, but that only lasted less than a month.'

How are your projectionists trained?
"There used to be a class at Napier University. It was Bill Smith who was in charge of that department. But, as the cinemas diminished, the apprentices diminished, and it wasn't worthwhile having the course. But I was very fortunate; my three projectionists went through Napier, so they have this terrific knowledge of projection and we bring our own apprentices in. We give them a fast track into projection, then, if they manage to get through the fast track – which is putting a film on the screen, making a film up – we give them another year of finer detail – watching sound, making sure the light is correct and all that. Then we give them a certificate at the end of two years. So that is how we work it now.'

Chapter 5

Sport and recreation

With not a single public tennis court, bowling green or football pitch you might think sport didn't interest the Morningside folk. But you would be wrong.

Tennis

Where did you play tennis?
'I didn't play a lot of tennis; I did play a bit at the Braids and I did play occasionally up at Plewlands, in the public park up there and you had to book your court. It was very popular in those days. You had to make sure you were up on time. They were quite good courts.'
Did you wear whites for your tennis? Did you have tennis shorts?
'Not at Plewlands, I think you could appear in anything up there. I think possibly at Mortonhall they wore whites usually.'
'You just played in plimsolls – at least I did, not in these thick soled shoes.'
'I don't think they existed then.'
What did the City Hospital nurses who were living in do in their spare time?
'Well I don't know about the nurses, I know about the sisters: we played tennis in the summer. We had a games hall where we played ping-pong and badminton. We held dances in the winter time.'

Skating

Do you remember skating on the tennis courts in winter?
'Yes we used to get up to Mortonhall. It was a very nice, quiet place.'

And someone mentioned skating on Blackford pond?
'Well, we went on it but we weren't actually skating. I was young at the time; I was just sliding on it.'
'But there was quite a lot of skating on the Blackford pond. We used to get annoyed when they broke chunks off the ice to let the ducks get to the water.'
'It was always so busy. It was even busier than the ice rinks in those days. That is something I did do – I used to go to the ice rink. That was something for Saturday morning entertainment.'

Walking

'In the summer we played tennis and went for walks. I remember when we went up to Swanston we walked up the Braidburn Valley and through a farm.'
'Harwell's farm, yes.'
'That farm used to have spaniels, Springer spaniels. You went through the Braidburn Valley, on and turn left up to the farm and on the right hand side of that there was a kennel with Springer spaniels.'
'You went on up the back, up a wee path that skirted round Comiston House, through the woods and you came out eventually beside the Caiystane. Then across Oxgangs Road and up to the Swanston Village.'
'And over the Pentlands to Flotterstone. We used to have tea there.'
'We used to walk our dog through there and I can remember when they started building in the Oxgangs area, coming right up to the Braidburn Park. We thought this was terrible.'
'On Edinburgh holidays, I would be coming back from Dumfries and there would be an extra bus put on at Biggar, and maybe another at West Linton and another that came to Flotterstone. This was for people who had taken the bus out to Colinton or Balerno, walked over the hills, standing queuing for the bus back.'
'Now walking over the Pentlands can't be the same because if they go to Flotterstone they've got to walk and then walk back to their car.'
'There are still a lot of people that walk though. It's surprising how many people there are out on the hills.'
'They've got the Ranger too, I mean it's encouraged.'

Riding

'I had a pony and I used to go riding on the Pentlands with the Pony Club. I remember well, up on the Pentlands, a girl fell off – a wee girl at this stage, seven or eight, something like that – and she was told, "Right, back on again!". The poor wee thing, tears running down. That was the only thing to do; you had to retain your confidence. But I remember this poor wee mite saying, "Oh, that's cruel!"'

Golf

If you didn't go dancing what were your leisure activities? Golf on the Braids?

'On the Braid Hills; golf was my major sport, I was an outdoor person.'

Did you learn to play golf up on the Braids? On number 1 or number 2?

'Both! And I joined Edinburgh Thistle Golf Club when I was about 17. I was a member of the BBs, and Alex McLaren, who was one of our officers, got me into Edinburgh Thistle Golf Club. Then I joined the Merchants of Edinburgh, just across from the City Hospital.'

'My grandfather was a founder member of the Merchants; my father was a member and a captain but never a champion. I walked round with my father when the top holes, and the hole across the road, were played; that was in the early thirties. There always was the lure of a high tea at the end; the club mistress was a brilliant baker. If mother was doing something, it wasn't difficult to persuade me to walk round with the prospect of bacon and egg and home made scones at the end.'

'My father always encouraged me and said that I had a good swing but, like most girls, I played tennis: tennis in the summer and badminton in the winter. Unfortunately the war came on while I was at school and everything came to a halt. There was no membership at the Merchants at that time and the ladies who were there just played along and kept things going because all the men were away.'

'It was in 1947 that I joined as a full member. I had to be over 18 as there was no Junior section for girls. My mother played there too; she was a restricted member but she attained a reasonable standard.'

'I had lessons from the professional, a Mr Allan. The secretary at that time was most insistent that you must learn the background to the game, become proficient and learn the rules. As someone who worked, I often could not start before 6pm and very rarely did I get finished.'

'When you got the hang of the rules then you could play in the medals. It was always dark. The only medals you could play in were June and July, sometimes in August, but September was a dead loss. We did feel very hard done by and some members left to play elsewhere.'

'I was a shorthand typist and I was very much an outsider as a working girl. Those who were the "morning" golfers were instrumental in getting a girls' junior membership started when their daughters were reaching the age when boys could be juniors. They were really quite right and they insisted; it was the mothers who applied the pressure.'

'There was a club for girls; I think they played on the Braids. There was a trophy for which they played. It was still going strong for some years. At the time, I was Captain or Vice-captain which puts it about 1970/1.'

'Changes have taken place over the years – some good, some not so good. In the past there was much more keenness and the Merchants could get three teams plus caddies to turn out for the Morrison Miller and people would be upset if you didn't call on them to be involved: that was the club. This is a different generation.'

'I think that in golf, as in bowls, women are still treated as second-class citizens. Some men in particular are very intolerant and very much against fair and equal treatment; quite held down on women. In fact, if it hadn't been for the ladies' clubs, the Merchants would have died. That certainly was the case during the Second World War.'

'During the war, ground was taken over at the 5th and 6th holes and the 6th has never really recovered from being dug up to "dig for victory".'

'There were sheep on the course on both sides of the road for a long time after the war, up to the fifties.'

'A wee story, which illustrates how much things have changed:

another member and I were playing in a recent medal and we were looking for a ball behind the 4th green when we overheard two ladies also playing in the medal. "Is this the 5th hole we are playing?" said one. "No, it's the 6th", said the other. Since, in fact, it was the 7th they could not have been paying much attention to what they were doing and I wonder what scores they would have put in! That would not have happened in the past as you had to know the rules and the etiquette.'

'The war was a considerable influence. Women had to wear trousers to do the work they had to do; they were often doing men's work and had to dress appropriately. When I first played golf, you wore your old clothes. It was a case of "That will do for golf". After clothes rationing stopped, there was a change with a greater availability of "casual" clothing.'

'The first clubs I bought were Gleneagles. You saved up for them and got them gradually. You got your driver and then, perhaps, a three wood and so on as you could afford them or were given them as presents. I just always had a half set. They cost a lot of money at £1 each at a time when you were earning £4 10s a week. Shoes were more important in some respects than the clubs; they had to be waterproof and, of course, a good waterproof jacket was an essential.'

'I was born in Edinburgh and I had a little bit of golf at school but afterwards I was really a tennis player and played along here in Eden Lane at a place called the Martins (a bowling green and tennis courts). I went there and played tennis.'

'1939/40 brought the war and there was nobody playing tennis. I had a friend who suggested I play golf – take a penny tram up the road. I took four or five clubs of my father's, which were hickory (he must have played golf), and went up to the Merchants and more or less pottered about with Jenny. Eventually my mother bought me a half set of golf clubs: that was 1943. I was called up and came back to the Merchants in August 1946 and that was when I started to play again.'

'I really didn't play seriously until 1977 when I went to Ballater, then I really became a golfer. I was told by fellow members to swing the club round my neck because I really was hockeying, having played hockey at school. It was in 1977 that I really got the idea of playing golf and, of course, with videos I have been enthusiastic about the technical side of golf.'

'I never had any instruction when I started, apart from the advice from my brother on the grip. That is why I went to the library and picked out a book by Pam Barton and of course followed her. It was the only measures I had. Ideally a lesson from the professional is very sound and the way it should be done. You can have your lesson and go off and practise. One of the regrets that I have is that I did not have access to a practice ground until four or five years ago.'

'Golf balls were very hard to get but there was a firm down in the south of England to whom you could send your balls and they came back as remoulds. My clubs were Thorntons so you could get additions/replacements – True Arc I think they were called.'

'My mother never played golf but I was very aware when we went on holiday to Aberdeen and went to the pitch-and-putt that she had a good eye. Women of my mother's vintage were never encouraged to take up sport. I am always sorry that when her friends took up indoor bowling at the Synod Hall (the place where all the indoor bowling was played on the floor below the cinema) my mother didn't.'

'It was 1953 when I joined Kilspindie and I had to be sponsored by two men. I did not know who to get but a Merchants colleague saw that there was no problem and my application went in in October. In December I received a letter confirming my membership and asking for an entry fee of £10. I turned to my father and said, "I haven't got £10". "Well," said he, "you will have to get £5 for your birthday in January and you can find the other £5." On a day in March or April I trundled down in my Morris 8 to find out where it was, pay my subscription and get my fixture card. Then had the most wonderful afternoon tea for 2s.'

'The Post Office had men's and ladies' clubs and that gave me a lot of outings and I had the chance to play for the Post Office at a wide range of courses. The club is now defunct although we have a dinner once a year.'

How did you manage to fit in your golf while you were working?
'It was really a matter of rushing up to the Merchants for the six o'clock draw and I did manage to play in the medals. I did have a few years on "flexi-time" which was a help. Playing at Kilspindie was another matter. I had to take a day's leave. I had to work that out very carefully. One of the things that I did go for at Kilspindie was to get the businesswoman the chance to play on a Sunday. That only came about five years ago.'
'I had to gear my life to meeting the playing times at the Merchants. Change will come and some men will have to measure up to the change. Women who take up golf do tend to take it quite seriously. They take the instruction and follow through in their commitment.'

Chapter 6

War

The war was of great significance in the lives of the group members. Here are some of their memories.

Evacuation

Were you at school in the war years?
'I was, but I was evacuated during the war, seven miles outside Edinburgh, to Newtongrange. I think probably I was sent there to let my mother work on the tramcars. My mother was a conductress on the 23. I don't think it was a very viable route because I think she let everybody off with their fares. But I didn't go to Morningside School until, well it must have been about '45 or '46, so I was nearer eight by that time.'
'I was evacuated too, to Nethy Bridge, but we didn't stay too long, probably a month. We all came back. My grandmother, who lived in Bruce Street, used to look on to the railway. I can remember us all going down to Waverley and my grandmother out the window, waving to us as though we'd never be coming back again. But, as I say, we were back in a very short time.'

Air raid shelters

'One of my friends was saying that there were air raid shelters in that piece of ground just at Hermitage there.'
Do you call that the Plantation?
'I think some people call it the Plantation.'
'I can never remember an air raid shelter being there but I remember the ones in the backgreens.'
What sort of shelters were these: Anderson?

'No, they were underground, really underground.'
'There was a concrete bit that came up and the door was there and you went down the steps but it had been excavated. Did you have that in Springvalley?'
'I think we must have, I only vaguely remember that. I remember the air raid shelters in George Watson's school because sometimes we used to go and play there.'
'There were big air raid shelters out here in the Plantation.'
'You went down steps to them, they were dug out, but the top of them was above ground level and there was turf over the top.'
'That's the type they had in the Meadows.'
'They would be re-enforced concrete.'
'I seem to remember people used to grow nasturtiums over these shelters.'
'There were quite a lot of air raid shelters in people's gardens.'
'Oh yes, Anderson shelters.'
'These shelters must have been left for a good few years after the war. They used to be tarred you know, the bit that sloped down and I can remember we used to slide from the top. We used to get a row for getting our pants, our breeks, all tar.'
'And I'll tell you they used to take up quite a bit of the drying green.'
'We were in the shelter occasionally if there was an air raid.'
'I was under the dining room table, I remember. What good that would have done I have no idea in retrospect, but my mother thought it was all right at the time.'
'We had a shelter in the backgreen in Springvalley. There was one shelter between two blocks and we've still got the gap in the green. The railings just go up so far and then you go through to the next green because that's where the shelter was. I can remember being taken out a couple of times but the houses in Springvalley were just a room and kitchen and a little box room off the kitchen which I slept in and, more often than not, everybody just came in there beside me. It was "Move over!" and we all cowered in there till the All Clear.'
'My mother put a big double bed in a big walk-in cupboard in the hall because there were no windows in it. I was the oldest; I had a younger brother and sister and we used to sit in there. We always

got chocolate cake so we thought this was great. Then we realised the gas main was in this cupboard. My mother had thought it was safe because there was no glass!'

'During the war, I remember we were involved in an air raid. I was taking my mother back about half past six or seven to hospital when the siren went and we were on the 41 bus. Of course we just had to get off the bus and get through the gates and up the drive. I was so impressed with the organisation. There were wardens out with torches and they got us in. We had to go into the bowels of the earth; there was a shelter there and the Matron and the Assistant Matron, were all down there with all the walking patients. It was very efficiently done. I was very impressed with them. I never worried about my mother.'

'You knew she was in good hands.'

Gas masks

'I remember the gas masks. Everybody had to carry them.'

'I remember when the sirens went off right at the beginning of the war just after it had been declared; I ran out into the street with my gas mask on.'

Air raids

'I think I remember the first air raid on Edinburgh. The shrapnel fell and we were out collecting it. The Germans were making for the Forth Bridge.'

'Was that 16 October 1939, the very first raid?'

'That's right, that was it.'

'Not the Clydebank blitz?'

'No no, that was later, '41.'

'But the Forth Bridge raid; there was no siren, that was the big problem.'

'At Morningside Station there was a big Police Box with a siren on top.'

Shrapnel and bullets

'The biggest fear or danger we had was when the Navy would start shooting from the Forth at planes flying over. But they were using ordinary shells, not anti-aircraft shells and there was a whole lot of them peppering in around the Hermitage. Just below our garden at Braid Hills, there were quite a few shell holes. We were at far more risk from the Navy shells going up and coming back down again. I remember going into the field which is now the top of the Hermitage and picking up shrapnel.'

'Oh I remember we used to hunt for shrapnel after a raid.'

'Yes I suppose, for boys particularly, it would be a marvellous thing to be able to keep a bit of shrapnel.'

'The shooting range was up on the Braids; firing up through the valley towards the club house. We used to go and dig in the bank there to get the bullets that had been fired at the targets.'

'I remember the Home Guard going out on exercises and you weren't allowed to go up the hill on a Sunday morning because they were out there.'

Bombings

'I remember coming home early evenings and looking out from Braid Hills Avenue towards the Forth Bridge to see if the barrage balloons were up. And it's astounding, years after the war, instinctively I looked across to see if the barrage balloons were there.'

'You would have a clear view.'

'Yes, as soon as you came down you could just look across towards the Bridge and see whether you were likely to have a raid tonight, whether the barrage balloons were up or not.'

'Of course the Braids was a decoy during the war for Edinburgh. If the Germans had bombed Edinburgh, the Braids would have gone up.'

'We had a serviceman billeted with us and he was part of the control team. If you are going across Braid Hills Road, where there's the first walkway down to the Hermitage, on the opposite side from there, there was a building, a Nissen hut type building built back into the hillside. That was the control centre for setting the Braids afire. There was a whole section from about there almost right down to Liberton which was shut off from the public, and that was full of oil barrels and detonating charges I suppose. This chap said: "Look, if the Germans bomb, for goodness sake get out of here because this is a very dangerous area. This is where they'll be setting as a pathfinder." They used to bomb with

incendiaries to start a fire and then the rest of the bombers would come in and bomb the fire area and so this was the decoy for Edinburgh.'
'That's why that building was built back into the hill.'

'Another thing I heard a while back that I had no knowledge of; when invasion was imminent they were afraid that London would be captured and the BBC would come to a halt. They had satellite-broadcasting stations set up all over the country and there was one in a house in Newbattle Terrace. [No.11] Apparently later owners had wondered why there was a concrete floor in their kitchen or basement and this had been where the studio was. They would have broadcast to the nation from this basement in Newbattle Terrace. It was never used but it was all equipped ready.'
'At least they had thought ahead.'
'Then the ponds at Happy Valley where you used to be able to skate at night, when they had the lights on; they were used during the war as cooling water. The factory there was overhauling engines for the Services and the water was used for cooling tanks for running these big American engines.'

'During the war St Hilary's school was taken over as an ARP station.'
'And some of South Morningside School was taken over too.'
'There were still a few classes went on.'
'Yes, but I know Dad was in charge of the ARP. The garage basically closed so he had time other than doing munitions work to earn some money.'
'Yes because no one could run their cars during the war.'
'He did munitions but he was in charge of the St Hilary's depot and Mum was an ambulance driver with them.'

'It's funny how you forget those things. I remember being on the buses. I am sure it was during the war because they were all blacked out, and as you got to Church Hill you thought, "Right! 1, 2". You counted the bus stops making sure you didn't go past your stop and quite often you did.'
'It would be trams.'

'Quite often you did go past your stop. If it didn't stop at one of the stops you miscounted and you were away up the road but it didn't matter, you walked home.'
'The conductors were quite good at shouting out the stops – or conductresses it would be mostly. The men were away at the war.'
'I remember there were people recruited to be auxiliary conductors. Businessmen on their way home took over the duties of conductor for a couple of hours or when they were going to work.'

'My brother was in the Scouts during the war, not here at Braid Church but at the one that's now the Church Hill Theatre. [Morningside High] They had huts in what's now called Cuddy Lane, round there. And my brother said it was great because all the leaders were away to the war and the boys really just ran their own Scout Troop. They used the hut all through the week not just whatever night the Scouts were.'
'I can remember my brother was in the Scouts too, but he was working as something to do with the ambulances. He was only about 13 and it was after the Clydebank blitz and they were cleaning the ambulances. The ambulances were all bloodstained and all these young boys were washing them out.'
'My brother was in the Auxiliary Fire Service and he was just a teenager.'

Rationing

'We forget that after the war you just couldn't buy new things. People had to keep their handbags for years and years and darn their gloves. We forget that the austerity went on for a long time after the war years.'
'I'm amazed when you hear it was away into the fifties before rationing stopped.'
'It was a long time before things began to be more available.'
'During the war there were allotments in the Braidburn Valley. My brother was a year at Morningside School before he went to Heriot's. They had an allotment there and my mother used to go up and dig it. She thought this was great because we were living in a flat. They were very popular for growing your own

vegetables.'
'I didn't live in Morningside at that time but across by the Meadows and it completely ruined my childhood as far as games were concerned. The whole of the Meadows was given over to allotments except for the bits that were air raid shelters, static water tanks or decontamination centres – there was hardly any playing space at all. It was incredible! I mean people don't realise how much of the Meadows was taken up with all this.'

'I can remember when I was a child, when you couldn't get ice cream during the war; Rossi's used to sell the cones with a spoonful of jelly in them. You got a jelly cone for a penny.'
'After the war Wall's ice cream came out in blocks and you had to queue for one each.'
'I also remember during the war the Store baker opposite Morningside School; on a Friday afternoon they used to get cake in – it was the only time they had it. You could get either a piece of Madeira cake or a piece of sultana cake and you had to queue and the queue was away down the street! Our job was to stand in the queue till our mother could come. We kept the place in the queue.'
'My 21st was held in Dunedin Hall in Morningside Drive. I was on leave from the Services. It had been booked and all the friends and aunts had been keeping the odd bits, you know; ration of this and ration of that, and it's amazing what was achieved. Mr Waugh, the butcher at that time, the only thing he could come up with was that he would see that I had a good main course. And we thought, "What on earth will turn up?" Well the only thing that could turn up was a beef steak pie.'
'But Waugh's beef steak pies were well known and you took the empty tin back.'
'I don't know how many beef steak pies were done but we had quite a nice time what with the Sunday School and half the Dramatic Club there, if they weren't in the Services, and all the relations and various people. The Dunedin Hall was a nice place for a party at one time. And that was a wartime party! Don't ask me what we had for pud!'
'Did you have a birthday cake?'
'That would be made by your father or mother. You didn't buy it.'

'Oh no, you would never dream of buying it.'
'It was the little bits of sugar and whatnot from various people.'
'Sharing the rations.'
'But it was very nice. You remember Young's the baker at the corner of Morningside Drive? Miss Thomson was the manageress and she had known me since pram days, so my 21st cake was given by courtesy of Young's with the family sugar. That was another place people had for parties. Nowadays they have this wonderful shop at Church Hill that gives parties for children.'
What about clothes rationing? You would be getting to the age, especially when you came back from the Forces, when you would be wanting some nice, new, fashionable clothes.
'Well, as it was all coupons and you just had your ration, you just had to cope. I was given a photograph recently of my father and mother and me at the wedding of a friend of the family in January 1952. Well, the fashions in this photograph! I didn't recognise any of us. There was I sitting in my demob coat which was utility, but it was the height of fashion at the time. I thought, after four years in khaki I wanted something bright so I had a cherry red coat. When we were demobbed, you see, the men were given a suit and a cardboard case; we were given coupons. So it was up to us.'
'I went to London and did a secretarial course. I then worked for a while in the Hammersmith Hospital and I can remember being quite a success because I was the first secretary in the hospital who had a New Look skirt. It was just slightly below the knee.'
'The height of fashion!'
'Absolutely, and it was flared. The nurses and female doctors and lab workers you didn't see out of uniform but we, of course, were not in any uniform and here we were: "Oh have you seen her, she's got a New Look skirt?" So that was my five minutes of glory!'
'We had a boost when we first came out because anything we had was at least four years old and out of fashion. I remember I was still stationed in Preston when my sister was to be married and I had to go into a shop and choose a hat I thought would go with a dress I knew I had at home that I was going to wear. Standing in a hat shop in Preston, in my uniform, trying on hats: it was ridiculous!'

Enlisting

You were in the Forces during the war. Can you remember joining up? Where did you go to sign on?

'We signed on at the Labour Exchange, down at Tollcross. You were called up and I said I wanted to be in the office and there was a test, an arithmetic test, and the girl said to me, I think she was a sergeant, "You haven't got any workings." I said, "No, it's mental arithmetic," and so it was. I did my stint in the services in the WAAF as a wireless operator. I went no further than England. I was sent to Gloucester first of all – that was your month's square bashing. Then I was sent up to Errol to wait for my posting. It was all cold water and concrete – it was horrible! The wireless training school was attended by British and Russian officers. The Russian officers did not speak English but they were always most polite. Then I went down to Blackpool for 20 months; I never wanted to see the place again! Then I was away down in Wiltshire, then Charterhall. I was never happy at Charterhall; it was too near home. Then down to Yorkshire, by jove, it can snow on the moors down there!"

'That was a long time.'

'Three and a half years.'

Were any others of you in the Forces?

'No, by that time I was expecting my first child or I would have been called up. My husband wasn't called up; he was on the railways so he was in a reserved occupation. He had to work very hard although he wasn't away; long hours, he never knew when he would be back. He had to go all over the place at one time but he was in Edinburgh.'

'No, much to my great disappointment. My mother wasn't very strong and I felt I couldn't volunteer. When I came to be called up I was exempt because they were short of stenographers in the civilian world. Anyway, I got a chance of going as a civilian to a liaison officer who liased with the regional commissioner for Civil Defence. It was very enlightening; correspondence with Lord Wavell and the Black Watch, but hard work.'

'I joined up before the war, because I joined the FANY's[First Aid Nursing Yeomanry] so I was there from then on. I didn't have to be. As a speech therapist I could have carried on working but you weren't going to do that! We carried on with the war.'

Casualties of war

'Someone told me a tale about the Astley Ainslie hospital where she was a nurse and, of course, if you go to the top of Blackford Hill you can look down on the hospital.

'It was an Army hospital during the war.'

'One nice summer evening she and a friend had taken a walk up to the top of Blackford Hill and they realised they could see all these soldiers down below on the verandahs.'

'Yes and the beds were all outside.'

'So they started waving and shouting to them and the soldiers started waving back and all of a sudden all the courting couples on Blackford Hill stood up from the bushes to see what was going on. The nurses at the top of the hill couldn't see this and it wasn't till the next morning when they were on duty, the soldiers told them that when they started shouting to them all the courting couples stood up to see what was wrong.'

'And the Princess Margaret Rose hospital, during the war, it was a hospital for the wounded soldiers.'

'That's right, they lived outside in the open – very healthy.'

'Yes, and remember the Astley Ainslie, you could see the beds from the Blackford Hill.'

'You could see them when you went along on the suburban train.'

'Yes it was full of wounded soldiers, wasn't it?'

VE day

'I was in the Air Force. I was stationed in Preston, I did what I suppose they call radar plotting. Then I was stationed, to my annoyance, in Edinburgh at Turnhouse. I didn't join the Air Force to just come home! We were closed down because by that time it was fighter and we weren't needed so much. I was to be sent to Inverness and one of the officers who was around at the time said, "Where are you going?" and I said, "Inverness." He said. "Oh that's ridiculous", and he went away out of the room, came back and said, "It's all right, I've got you stationed at Turnhouse." I could have murdered him! However I worked there with Flying

Control and then I was sent to South Wales; that was great fun. I was still at Turnhouse at VE day because I was sent up for a Commission Board, skipped out of camp the day before and went off to London. Standing around on the train as usual (it was absolutely packed; it was a night train), kit bags and all that,we kept seeing lights everywhere. We couldn't understand it. So when we arrived in London we discovered it was VE day.'

You didn't know?

'No, we got on the train not knowing. I enjoyed VE day in London; joined all the crowds, went to Buckingham Palace and everything else, shot around the streets and had great fun. Then I had the Commission Board the next day and they said, "How do you feel about it?" and I said, "Well, it's rather different now!"'

VE night on Princes Street

'I remember on VE night, going down to Princes Street.'

'Oh yes, I think everyone was in Princes Street!'

'The switch-on of the floodlights on the Castle.'

'Fantastic. Magic!'

'We all had flags. We had flags at our gate post: the Union Jack.'

'I remember having red, white and blue ribbon in my pigtails. It was beautiful ribbon. My mother had got it from her sister-in-law who probably had it from the last war. It was beautiful quality ribbon and I had thick hair then. There was a little kid up the street who was just a sitting-up baby in her pram and she had a red, white and blue ribbon on too, and she hadn't a hair on her head but she had her red, white and blue ribbon on!'

Chapter 7

Transport

It was inevitable that we would get round to talking about transport and traffic.

Cars

Tell us about your father's business, the garage business. When was it established?

'Well, he started in 1919 when he came out of the Army from the First War and went into Balcarres Street. There's a pend – well it's now built on – on the left-hand side just as you go along Balcarres Street.

I think Forrest was the builder who built this yard and my father got a couple of sheds in there as his initial set-up. He worked from there until he built the first bit of the Braid Road garage in 1922.'

So what was there – just an empty space?

'It was an old church yard.'

That's where the tin church was?

'That's one of the tin churches. St. Ninians' church was where the garage was. One of the mechanics in the garage who lived in Comiston Terrace remembered, as a boy, playing on the remains of the church before the garage was built.'

And what sort of trade did your father have then?

'Well, I have some knowledge of that. Actually, I've still got my father's first ledger from the garage side of it – no, I think I might even have the ledger going back to Balcarres Street. He was going out buying things for people and repairing them. It was cars or motor bikes or anything with wheels!'

Do you have a record of petrol prices?

'Well, they were high, well, relatively speaking. In 1919, a gallon of BP petrol was 3s 7d – an awful lot of money at that time. I can remember when we lived up at Braid Hills Avenue, the next-door neighbour had a Rolls and chauffeur. She said (I'm now talking in, I suppose the late 1940s, early 1950s, that sort of time, or it might have even been a bit later than that) "When petrol gets to 5s a gallon, the chauffeur has to go!" The cheapest Dad sold petrol at in Braid Road was 10d a gallon. It was ROP petrol – Russian Oil Product.'

Was it sold in cans?

'By that time, I think he might have had it in pumps. It was previously in cans, but he had, I think, the second pump in Edinburgh, just inside the door. Rossleigh had the first one.'

Were there businesses that had motorised transport in those days? I mean vans.

'Oh yes, but not so many local shopkeepers running a van.'

'It was a boy with a bike.'

'A boy with a bike; and you'd get old Mr Sinclair, I don't know if you remember him, old Mr Sinclair, the grocer, riding around after he shut the shop. He would go all around doing his deliveries. But later on Jim Grosset had a wee mini van which was sold to the Seths, the market gardener in Ethel Terrace.'

What were the popular cars when you first started working in the garage – what makes?

'Oh well, there were the Swifts, the popular Austin, Morris, Ford, Vauxhall and Hillman. They were the main popular cars, but there were plenty of the others: Armstrong Siddeleys and Daimlers and other names that have disappeared – Sunbeams, Talbots.'

'It always amazes me nowadays, because when I was a child, I used to be allowed to stand on the running-board and hang on to the car while it was being driven along, presumably not at a great speed, but we thought it was great. Imagine doing that now!'

'My doctor practised from Cluny Drive, the house next to the church, the house on the corner. He had a series of old Rolls Royces that he used to use and he was a keen sailing man as well.'

So did you father look after the Rolls Royces?

'Oh yes, I had many a row over these Rolls Royces when I was a youngster.'

'One of these daft motoring stories about our doctor was that he had this old 1922 Rolls which we had to keep on the road for him. He would come up through Glenlockhart and at the crest of the hill, at the Poor House there, switch the engine off – down the hill, along Greenbank Drive, out onto Comiston Road, down Comiston Road, up Comiston Place, across Braid Road and freewheel into his drive. That was his normal!'

Were you aware that in the 1970s more and more people had cars, and cars were changing?

'Oh yes, wealth brought constant change in cars, but the usage changed tremendously from this time. It would be pandemonium because all the cars that had been laid up for six months over the winter would now be getting out and onto the road. It was a lot of hard work at this time, getting people back on for the summer because cars, prior to that, were just for pleasure. They weren't a working tool as they are nowadays.'

Were you very young, when you learned to drive?

'Ah well, to be truthful, I drove down to the City Chambers on my 17th birthday to get my driving licence. I didn't have to have a test at that stage just after the war. So I've never had a driving test yet apart from the Service ones.'

Having driven in the Services excused you?

'No, no, it was because during the war there was no testing, naturally, and it was into the late 1940s, early 1950s before they started testing drivers again. There was a big block of people to whom they said,"Well, if you've been driving for four or five years, you're alright."

'Well, I was one of them. I had been driving and then I was advised to sit a test in 1950. That was the start of them.'

'That's interesting, I took my test in the mid 1950s, I didn't realise there had been no tests in that period.'

'Dad was driving before there were driving licences. It was about 1905–1906, somewhere about that, and you had to be 14 to get a driving licence. My grandfather had bought a car – a char-à-banc type, like a six-seater car, I think it was – and Dad was driving it when he was about 13, and the local policeman had said, "Right, the new law has come out, you've got to have a driving licence and you've got to be 14. But you're such a good driver, you're a far better driver than most of the men around here, so long as you stay in my patch, I'm not going to see you."'

Do you still have the old cars?

'Yes, oh yes, still got the old steam car and the Sunbeam Talbot that my father used to drive as well. We were out this weekend up to Crieff, there was a Sunbeam Talbots owners' meeting.'

And is it running beautifully?

'It's not too bad. It's now 50 years old itself.'

'Your father taught me to service my car. I used to do my own servicing with him standing behind my shoulder, and I used to come up and see him driving his steam car.'

'I've still got it. I've just discovered I've got a major job. I tried steaming it yesterday and there was a whooshing noise and I realised the boiler's got a hole in it.'

'You've still got it! Do you run it then?'

'Well, there's a steam car run this year up in Aberdeenshire, I was intending to take it, I don't know now.'

'My husband kept his car in a lock-up along at Pettigrew's garage in Jordan Lane. He was a civil engineer and the staff dance was always held in one of the big hotels in Glasgow. What happened was we took a taxi to the Mound, and a bus picked us up because nobody was allowed to drink and drive, and they always had a couple of hours free drinking before the meal. I said to my husband, "Have you booked that taxi?" and he said, "Oh no, I'll see Willie Pettigrew". So the next day he said, "Too late now", and I said, "I knew! I kept telling you I wanted to book it." He says, "It's alright, Willie's lending us a hearse." So I said, "I'm not going in a hearse, for goodness sake!" And he said, "It's alright, you can get up at the front with the driver and I'll go in the back."

I said, "Certainly not! If you think I'm coming out in Morningside Road in a long dress, – I'll lie down in the back!" And he said, "Don't be so silly, the taxi was booked ages ago!"'

'I had a similar experience: I was going to a ball in the Caley Hotel and it was a long-dress thing. I had booked a taxi and it didn't come. I couldn't get another one and the only person I knew with transport was my mother's neighbour's son-in-law, who was a painter and decorator, and I arrived at the Caley Hotel in the painter and decorator's van.'

'We had a Nissan for many years and it very rarely broke down. It was wonderful. I've just given it up; it was quite old. We had no garage up in Comiston Road, and after days of frost it would just start up magnificently. If that had been an Austin as we had had in earlier days, it would never have started without the AA man.'

'I wasn't a car owner, not until I came to Edinburgh. But here, I used to go to work by car. That was one thing I was thinking about the difference in the traffic. When you look out at this new [2001] set-up at Morningside Station! When I first started driving up and down, there were no traffic lights at all at the junction. Nothing – it was just a general free-for-all.'

'There weren't the same number of cars around and I don't remember it being a terrible problem. You had to watch what you were doing, but there was no sense of being caught in a mass of traffic; it just wasn't there. Now if there are no traffic lights, it's bedlam.'

Horses

'There were quite a lot of horses still trotting around.'

'Making deliveries, like the milk horse.'

'Maxwell Street, well there was the coal depot at the end of Maxwell Street and all the coal merchants used to come along with their horses. Some had lorries.'

'A lot of the men used to go to Bennet's pub and come out in an awful state, but you know, to be fair to the men, they took their horses down to the stables away down in Cluny Place, along the Nile Grove and along by the railway.'

'Oh, were these stables? In later years, they were garages and I often wondered what they had been before because they are big – they didn't look as if they had been built as garages.'

'Yes, Cluny Place, right by the railway down at the bottom of the hill. Many a time I delivered papers at 6 o'clock at night and this guy was taking his horse down there. He was very drunk, but the horse was looked after.'

'This is my point; these men had hearts of gold when it came to their animals.'

'They were very patient animals. You used to see them standing –

the milkman's horse, the coalman's horse.'
'In fact they used to know their route themselves. Very often the milkman got off to deliver and the horse just moved on itself to the next station.'
'Of course the Canny Man, Mr Kerr, his grandfather and father, they both had pony and traps. The two generations both had pony and traps. I don't remember the grandfather, but they said Mr Kerr was an absolute demon when he drove about in the pony and trap and his father had had it before him. He drove it for quite a long time. There was quite a lot of traffic on the roads.'
Where would they keep them?
'Round the back, and there was a field at Church Hill, a road that you couldn't go down, and that was used for the horses.'
'The other family who was very interested in horses was our doctor's family. The children were of our generation and used to go riding on the Pentlands.'

Bus trips
'Was it Hunter's buses that went out to the waterworks? And then I think it was the SMT.'
'I remember the SMT buses going out to Penicuik and West Linton and so on.'
'There used to be bus tours – the furthest distance was Carlops. It was quite a good journey. I don't know if you got tea there. I can't remember. My mother liked these bus tours. That's about as far as they went. I suppose it would be the early 1930s or late 1920s.'
'She probably would get tea. There would be a little teashop.'
'Flotterstone was always busy, and the Dumfries bus went that way. It was Harper – Harper's bus.'
'Harper, that was before the SMT.'
'Do you remember the number 9 bus? George and Bobby, the driver and the conductor? In the school holidays we used to go up to Greenbank Row and get the number nine bus to Davidson's Mains for a penny.'

Suburban railway
Does anyone remember the suburban railway?
'Oh yes, we lived with it, it was wonderful!'

'I finished school at the end of fifth year and I was too young to start my nursery training so I worked in an insurance office in town. Because I was under 18, we filled in what we called a pink slip every week, and for a shilling (5p) a week, we used to go in the morning, come home at lunch time, go back after lunch, and then come home at night. This was all for a shilling.'

'I used to travel on the suburban railway too. I can't remember how much it cost, this would be in the 1950s and I used to come home for my lunch as well. I worked near Haymarket. The little café just next door to Sherry's, it used to be called The Neuk – the Dolphin, is it? They had old-fashioned pictures all round the wall, and there was one of people coming up out of the suburban railway. I am sure I am in the picture.'

'I used to get the suburban railway to the Waverley and you were probably only saving about 1d or 2d a week, which was a lot of money then, and I used to take it to the Waverley. I loved the train.'

'I used to go on the suburban railway to go to work. I used to work in the Scotsman office – 13 minutes from Morningside to the Waverley.'

'Yes, the train took you across country in one vehicle whereas if you went by bus, you always had to take two. There was never a cross-country bus until the 38 came along.'

Trams

Do you remember when they used to put luggage and things on the front of the tram – beside the driver, if you had a bike or anything?

'We used to put our Christmas tree up in the front of the tram. There was a long space between the driver and the stairs; a very high empty space, and we could get an eight-foot Christmas tree in there. On Christmas Eve we used to bring it up from Market Street.'

'The tramcars were good, you could put the pram on the front where the driver was and they put the chain across.'

'Now we were talking about that the other day, and a lady said that you left the baby in the pram. I was quite sure you took the baby out and took it in with you, surely!'

'You know, I can't remember. I think you would.'

'I can remember a mother with a baby under her arm and a rug

round it, running round the back to get on – mostly at the terminus.'
'At Braid Hills Road, that was the terminus.'
'And do you remember the wee hut there? That was the terminus.'
'It's still there.'
'Then they went from Braid Hills Road right up to Fairmilehead. Oh, it was a long journey on the tram!'
'One of my sort of memories was the lights in pairs, we were talking about this the other day; I think the 23 was green and orange or orange and green. I might be wrong but you got to know and, I think, the 15 was maybe red and white – one of them was red and white. 'The 11 was red and white.' 'Was it the 11?'
'Yes, I remember that one.'
'You see when you were standing in Princes Street at night time on one of those island things, that was when it was super; you could see the lights on the front of your trams coming along.'
'But it was strange when the buses came and you had to wait until you could see the numbers – which had to be a bit nearer – they were nearly on you before you could see the numbers.'
'I used to like to watch the sparks from the wire thing. I have a childhood memory of it.'
'However, it's a myth that there were no traffic jams then because I have photographs of Princes Street and Morningside Road with trams all going in one direction. Of course, they couldn't overtake, so the trams were just there and if, for some reason, one of them had broken down … or an accident, there was no way past the other trams. So it is a little bit of nostalgia attached to how smoothly Edinburgh flowed with the trams because it isn't true. You could have half a mile of trams with the road completely empty on either side because there were no cars but the trams couldn't move out and overtake.
'It was certainly handy if you were running for a tram; you could still jump on, they were going so slowly, you could jump on and off whenever you wanted. The doors didn't just close on you. In fact they didn't have doors, did they? It was open at either end.'
You mentioned the conductors; they played quite an important role, didn't they?
'They controlled the passengers and allowed so many on and so many upstairs or whatever. They were quite a bonus. For any

elderly or infirm person, or a mother with a child, the conductor was always there to help them on and off whereas now there is one driver who has to do everything – he just can't help anyone. The conductors were really very good.'

'I do remember when the points used to freeze and the traffic just came to a total standstill and everybody walked from Fairmilehead down to school and into work.'

'There was a man who used to ski around here in the winter. He wore very few clothes. Well, he wore a vest and tracksuit bottoms. Do you remember him?'

So, when you first came to Greenbank, the trams had stopped?

'Oh, the trams were stopped. The buses were running and it's interesting of course, in those days, a lot of people came home for lunch. Even on the bus, I got a 16 bus; I had an hour and a half. I worked in George Street.'

Did the bus go up Greenbank Crescent then?

'Oh yes, by the time we moved in 1958 the 41 was still going up Greenbank Lane, but we didn't use that bus, the 16 was in operation.'

'The 41 terminus was Greenbank Row.'

'We were talking about having hours for lunch – I used to travel home from Pitt Street, away down over Hanover Street, to come home for lunch! Up on the top deck; I sat and knitted.'

Foreign travel

When did you first go abroad?

'1955 was the first time I went abroad. It was on my honeymoon. We went to Northern France, to Sable d'Or, near Mont Saint-Michel.'

'I went abroad when my son and his wife got married and got a job in Brussels. Naturally, when they got settled we went to visit. That was very interesting because it was our first visit abroad, and to go on the flight was really quite something! We've had many visits since, and then they took us to Paris, which was another experience for us. We enjoyed that.'

'I went abroad during the war. I did nursing service, and went out to India. That was the first time – apart from England – if you can count that as a foreign country!'

'I went with the Holiday Fellowship to Switzerland in 1953, I think, and the next year we moved to Austria. We walked quite a lot over the mountains, up on the mountain railways and so on.'

'I think it was 1955 I went to Austria with a group, not specifically to go walking, but that was quite a bit of it.'

'The first time I went away was at 17. We went on a cruise to Norway. It was great fun being abroad, just the two of us.'

Chapter 8

Around and about

When locals think of Morningside, they almost always think of its churches and its clock, which is a significant focal point. This came out in our meetings.

Morningside Station

'Of course, Morningside Station was a very focal point with the clock in the middle. I always had a soft spot for that clock and, in some ways, had a lot to do with it because my father was manager of James Ritchie's – the clock people who were responsible for all the city clocks. So, instead of sending out the regulators to make sure it was alright, when he came home at night and in the morning, he used to go out with the stop watch, and look at the clock and then they didn't have to send anybody out at one in the morning to put it right when all the city clocks had to be changed. It was a treat, when I was a little older, to go and watch it being wound –all the mechanism came up from underneath the ground.'

'I just wonder if our clock is coming back and where it is going to be situated.'

'I think it is to be situated on the pavement on the side of the road; the east side of the road, where they have been building the pavement out, just above the little hut. So it will be back and it will face North and South, the same direction as it has always done.'

[Clock now placed in position – since end of 2001.]

'Lovely, I do miss it. I always look for the time when I come down in the bus.'

'Yes, it's such a focal point in the area, I think everyone has been missing it.'

The churches

'There were a good number of churches in Morningside: seven or eight between Church Hill and Morningside Station, but several of them have now closed or been united with one of the others, so we've been left with all these beautiful church buildings. We were talking about the kind of uses they have been put to. First of all, Morningside High; that's now the Church Hill Theatre.'

You said you were a member of Morningside High Church. How did you feel when it became the theatre? Did you go to the little theatre much?

'I think it has been a good amenity for the area. It is mostly amateur companies that use it. I liked the pantomimes they did there; that was the Edinburgh People's Theatre. They still put on their pantomime every Christmas. I always felt that they stuck to the story that the children knew. It was good family entertainment.'

What about some of the other churches?

'Well, of course the Parish Church is now owned by Napier University.'

'Yes, I thought originally it was to be used for ceremonies, graduations, but I see students coming in and out regularly, so they must be using it for lectures.'

'Yes, they've improved the acoustics and they now do use it for lectures; it's a much better set-up than it was. I haven't been in it since it was reorganised; I'd like to have a look at it.'

'And then St Matthew's – it's now Cluny.'

'Yes, and it united – a long time ago now – with what was South Morningside. That's the one that was converted and is used as a church centre.'

'That's where we go for our keep-fit. Other things take place in Cluny Church Centre. At the moment, South Morningside School is so overcrowded that they have two P1 classes housed in Cluny Church Centre, and there is a local play group, a mother and toddler group and a ladies' slimming class, and I don't know what else.'

Do you know about the proposed union between this Church [Morningside Braid] and St Matthew's, which is now Cluny?

'Well, it was St Matthew's in my day. They're proposing to join them, are they? They were always great rivals!'

'This has happened because George Munro, who was the Minister at Cluny, has retired and they felt that because both congregations were dwindling and the two churches were so close together that they should unite, and that has been agreed.'
'Have they decided which church they are going to keep?'
'No! That is the million dollar question!'
'It's always a big problem!'
Tell us about Shopabreak. That's a Morningside Braid activity and a feature of life in Morningside.
'Well, Wednesday morning is Borestone. That was the Parish Church coffee morning, and they kept it going when they joined [Morningside Parish Church and Braid Church]; so they do Wednesday morning, and Shopabreak is Friday. But they have now stopped us baking for Shopabreak.'
Is this part of EEC rules or something?
'Food has to be cooked on the premises. You would have to do the baking in our kitchen, not do it at home and bring it in. Even with that, we would have to have a qualified person supervising.
It was a lot of work. I was doing about seven different things, everyone was, and it was a lot of baking. Now it is just biscuits.'
What was the idea behind Shopabreak; why did you start running it?
'Well, as far as I remember, it started originally as just tea and biscuits, in some place where people could come and meet, but then it did become rather a fund raiser. We gave quite a bit to the church.'
What about other churches?
'The Baptist Church is a lovely one.'
'Yes, that's the one that had the bad fire, up at Holy Corner.'
'Next to Luca's, it seems terrible that we say, "Next to Luca's" instead of saying that Luca's is next to the church! We seem to have got things slightly round the wrong way.'
'It was gutted by fire – I think it would be in the seventies – and they created a new cross out of the charred wood that they rescued and that's on the front of the building.'
'St Peter's Church is a beautiful church.'
'It is: a tremendous history there. But they are all well used in different ways, perhaps not all for worship now.'
'The Eric Liddell Centre, that was North Morningside Parish:

again, they've done a wonderful conversion of that building. They've filled in various levels above. There's one area which is a lovely little chapel, and then, right on the top floor, it's like a gymnasium; there's a big hall and shower facilities.'

'I don't know whether they have functions in that hall. I've been to coffee mornings and meetings, Abbeyfield meetings there and jumble sales.'

'I remember they used to roll out a red carpet and put up a canopy for weddings at North Morningside, and there was always a "pour oot" when the bride and groom left the church. There always seemed to be more children in those days. Certainly families were bigger.'

'What's the church opposite that, the one that's just had its roof redone?'

'That's called Morningside United, on the other side of Chamberlain Road. It was a Congregational Church and it united with North Morningside. It is known as Morningside United. It has a funny little porchway on the corner.'

'Yes, it's extraordinary architecture altogether. It is almost Spanish.'

'It doesn't look unlike St Peter's actually, the sort of square Mediterranean type.'

'The Church of England church across the road hasn't changed at all, hardly at all.'

Other buildings

'That bank is a lovely building at Holy Corner. I suppose, at one time, the manager would live on the upper floor there, in the house. And that house at the corner at Cluny Gardens, it's known as the Bank House.'

'Yes, that's right, it was the bank manager's house.'

'They used to do that didn't they? A lot of the banks had a flat up above for the manager.'

'And did something not end up at the entrance to Greenbank Park [Braidburn Valley]?'

'Oh, I think the gates came from Comiston House which, I think, went back to the early eighteenth century; it was built by an advocate who later became a Lord Provost. It's at the end of Camus Avenue. It's now turned into flats, but that was Comiston

House. It [Comiston] was a big estate and the gates were actually at the end of Camus Avenue where it joins the main road and they are the gates that are at the Braidburn Valley.'
'Am I right in thinking that Comiston House was a little hotel?'
'Yes, that's right, it had various owners over the years. At one stage, it was a small private hotel with residents; elderly, wealthy ladies and then it changed hands a few times and was more open to the public after that.'
'I remember my father and I went to look at this house for sale in Falcon Avenue and in the garden there was this object. "Oh", the owner said, "It's from the days when we used to go dancing. It's a bit of the Plaza." '
'Had they taken some of the bricks?'
'I thought it was more of an iron thing. It was maybe at the end of a staircase or something, you know? A wrought iron sort of thing, and they had stuck it in the middle of the garden. The wife was apologising for it!'
'Was that on the opposite side of the road from the Plaza?'
'Yes.'

Green space

'The little garden out in front of Morningside Braid Church; it's lovely when all the crocuses are out. It was the Brownies from Morningside Braid Church who planted these crocuses, wasn't it? They make a lovely splash of colour, and the trees too when the chestnut trees are in blossom. It is a lovely little garden. Who does it belong to?'
'Well, it actually belongs to the residents in Hermitage Terrace.'
'Do they have keys to get into it?'
'No, it isn't locked; it is very much open to the public. But, yes, they own it and the city maintains it after a fashion.'
'Do the public actually go in there?'
'Well, they do, which annoys me; they take a short cut by climbing over the fence to get to the bus stop.'
'They've trampled down all the new netting which was put round. In some places it has been removed completely. I saw a young man climb the fence and walk over the crocuses to get to the bus stop.'

'That patch of greenery at Hermitage Terrace is very neglected.'
'Well I always blamed the Council for not cutting the grass, but I believe it's the householders.'
'Actually, the houses there all owned a share of that and it was in the title deeds when you bought it and you paid up your share for the grass cutting and it was beautifully kept. But when it became more of a public area, and houses were being sold for other than residential, people didn't want to have that, and it was jointly agreed that 50 per cent of the up-keep would be paid by the title deed holders and 50 per cent by the Town. So the Town cut the grass twice a year, and the owners were supposed to do the rest, and that fell flat and now it has just gone until it's a mess.'

'They've produced a leaflet recently about the Braid Burn. They have done a lot of work in the Braidburn Valley and the leaflet describes the course of the burn and the wildlife and plants, and all the things you see along the way, bringing things up to date again because it was a bit neglected for long enough.'
'Of course there are very many more houses beyond that now. It was all park before; you used to walk up through Comiston Farm to Hunter's Tryst.'

'We realise that many features of Morningside, like the Old School House, now used for worship and other functions, have been omitted. Perhaps one day someone else will produce Volume 3'